Teen Ment

Survive Your Mood.
Survive Your Emotion.

Emily Grace

© Copyright 2023 - All rights reserved.

The content contained within this book may not be reproduced, duplicated or transmitted without direct written permission from the author or the publisher.

Under no circumstances will any blame or legal responsibility be held against the publisher, or author, for any damages, reparation, or monetary loss due to the information contained within this book, either directly or indirectly.

Legal Notice:

This book is copyright protected. It is only for personal use. You cannot amend, distribute, sell, use, quote or paraphrase any part, or the content within this book, without the consent of the author or publisher.

Disclaimer Notice:

Please note the information contained within this document is for educational and entertainment purposes only. All effort has been executed to present accurate, up to date, reliable, complete information. No warranties of any kind are declared or implied. Readers acknowledge that the author is not engaged in the rendering of legal, financial, medical or professional advice. The content within this book has been derived from various sources. Please consult a licensed professional before attempting any techniques outlined in this book.

By reading this document, the reader agrees that under no circumstances is the author responsible for any losses, direct or indirect, that are incurred as a result of the use of the information contained within this document, including, but not limited to, errors, omissions, or inaccuracies.

TABLE OF CONTENTS

INTRODUCTION 1
  The Road to Good Mental Health 1
    Part One 2
    Part Two 3

CHAPTER 1: TEENAGE TROUBLES 4
  It's Not Just You 4
    One in Seven 5
  Your Formative Years 7
    Body and Biology 8
    Social Struggles 9
    Emotional Crisis 10
  Today's Generation 12
    Once in a Lifetime 13
    Mental Health Matters 14

CHAPTER 2: ALL ABOUT ANXIETY 15
  Busy Head 15
    Signs and Symptoms 16
    Adolescent Anxiety 17
  Stressing Out 18
    Disorders and Triggers 19
      Social Anxiety Disorder 19
      Generalized Anxiety Disorder 20

Pressure and Perception 21
   Perfectionism 22
   Costly Consequences 23

CHAPTER 3: DEPRESSION, MOOD SWINGS, AND BURNOUT 25

When You're Not Just Moody 26
   Defining Depression 26
   Finding a Cause 28
      Life 29
      Chemistry 29

Mania and Other Moods 30
   Mania 30
   Bipolar Disorder 31

Burnout 32
   Trying Hard Enough 34

CHAPTER 4: NEURODIVERSITY 35

Not Neurotypical 35
   No Such Thing as Normal 36

Self-Identification 37
   The Umbrella 38

Attention and Activity 39
   Difficulties of Neurodiversity 40
      Focus 40
      Impulse 41

    Diagnosis 42
CHAPTER 5: IDENTITY: WHO AM I? 44
    Trying It On 45
        An Amalgamation 45
        Identity Distress 47
    Defining Personality 47
        Types and Traits..48
            The Big Five 48
            Types A, B, C, and D 49
            Myers-Briggs 50
        The Challenge of Personality 50
            Personality Disorders 51
    Existential Crisis 53
        Letting Go 54
        Purpose 55
CHAPTER 6: GENDER VERSUS SEX 56
    Transcending Gender 57
        Gender Dysphoria 57
            Signs and Symptoms 58
        Fluidity of Gender 59
        Gender Affirmation..60
    Who You Love..62
        Born This Way...62
        Sexuality Spectrum 63

Being Queer 64
Coming Out 65

CHAPTER 7: SELF-ESTEEM 67

The Foundation 67
    Your Origin Story 68
        Criticism and Praise 69
        Parenting Styles.. 70
Thinking Disorder 71
    High Expectations 72
    Self-Fulfilling Prophecy 72
    Feeling Incapable 73
    Mistreatment 73
The Only Way Forward 74
    Resilience.. 75
    Building Self-Esteem 76

CHAPTER 8: BODY, EATING, EXERCISE 78

Body Image... 78
    Influence(r)s... 79
    Distortion 80
    Dysmorphia.. 81
Eating Disorders 82
    Overlapping Features 82
    Compulsion 84
You Are Not in Control... 85

Hard Truth 86

CHAPTER 9: RELATIONSHIPS, SEX, AND SOCIAL MEDIA 88

Clashes 88
    Honesty 89
    Safe Haven 90

Peers and Popularity 91
    Finding Your People 92

Romance 93
    Virginity 94
    Safe Sex 95
    Avoiding Toxicity 96

Social Media 97
    Pros and Cons 97
    Discernment 98

CHAPTER 10: SELF-HARM 100

Driving Forces 100
    Self-Destruction 101
    Punishment 102
    Control 102
    Expression 103

Unsustainable 103
    Survival Strategy 104
    Dangerous Addiction 105

Stigma and Shame..106
   A Different Perspective 107
   Alternatives..108

CHAPTER 11: THE FIRST STEP: TALK TO SOMEONE..109

Speaking Up...109
   An Unbearable Weight..................................110
Trusted Sources..111
   Back Up Plans...112
   How Are You?...113
Sensitive Conversations 114
   Preparation..114
   Expectation 116

CHAPTER 12: GETTING HELP......................117

Seeing Someone...117
   A Little Faith...118
   One Step at a Time.......................................119
Practical Steps..120
   The First Appointment 121
Therapy..122
   Beginnings 123
   All of the Acronyms.....................................124
Additional Avenues..125
   Medication 126

    Caveats 126

    Intensive Treatment 127

CHAPTER 13: HELPING YOURSELF 129

    Taking Responsibility 129

        The Importance of Agency 130

    Basic Wellness 131

        Movement 131

        Food 132

        Sleep 132

        People 133

        Self-Care 133

    Healthy Coping 134

        Emotional Regulation 135

        Distress Tolerance 135

        Impulse Control 137

    Personal Growth 138

        Creativity 138

        Acceptance 139

        Mindfulness 139

        Positivity 140

CHAPTER 14: A NOTE TO PARENTS 141

    Warning Signs 141

        Degree of Change 142

        Taking Action 143

Starting a Conversation 144
    Reactions 145
    Next Steps 146
Creating a Culture 147
    All in This Together 148
    Validating Space 149

CONCLUSION **151**
Recap 151
GLOSSARY **153**
REFERENCES **155**
Image References 161

Trigger warning:
This book includes mention and discussion of sensitive topics around mental health such as anxiety, depression, identity issues, body image, eating disorders, bullying, substance abuse, addiction, self-harm, and suicide.

INTRODUCTION

Have you ever wondered if there might be something wrong with you? Do you have thoughts and feelings that you don't understand and can't control? Are you struggling with who you are? Do you feel scared, overwhelmed, and sad all of the time? Do you wish things were different? Do you feel like quitting and giving up?

You are not alone.

Mental health challenges are common, especially among people your age, and you do not have to suffer in silence. You do not have to feel ashamed, guilty, or confused. You are not broken, and you have not done anything wrong.

Most of all, there is a way out of the dark place you find yourself in, and there is understanding, help, and hope out there. You are worthy and capable of happiness.

The Road to Good Mental Health

This book is going to help you understand what you are going through. It explains different mental health conditions and symptoms, and explores all the various factors that could be affecting your mood, well-being, happiness, and health during this time of your life.

Moreover, this book shines a light on what to do next. It encourages you to speak out about your struggles and to get help for your feelings, thoughts, and behaviors. It provides step-by-step instructions for how to have uncomfortable conversations, get professional guidance, and improve your own mental health.

Part One

Being a teenager comes with a range of new challenges, and many can seem overwhelming and unmanageable. The first step to good mental health is understanding what you are struggling with, and we will explore all the different possibilities in the first 10 chapters of this book.

You might be experiencing the symptoms of a clinical mental illness such as anxiety, depression, or bipolar disorder. You may be struggling with neurodiversity or questions of identity. Who are you? Why are you different?

Many teens battle to come to terms with their gender identity and sexual orientation, and low self-esteem is a problem that underpins many mental health challenges. You might be suffering from disordered eating or an unhealthy relationship with your body. Moreover, adolescent relationships pose unique challenges, and you will likely have concerns about friendship, love, and sex.

Lastly, you may be struggling with self-harming, risky, and self-destructive behaviors, so we will look at these issues in more detail as well.

Part Two

The final four chapters of this book are about how to deal with your mental health challenges—actively and practically.

You should talk to someone you trust about your thoughts and feelings, and can consider getting professional help in the form of therapy or medication. You also have a lot of power to help yourself feel better through lifestyle changes, self-care, and healthy coping strategies.

Ultimately, it is possible to improve your mental health, and you will not feel this way forever. Once you start to understand what you are going through, you can learn how to cope with what you find challenging. Remember: You are worthy of happiness—don't give up on it.

CHAPTER 1

Teenage Troubles

Adolescence is a time full of transition, adaptation, and change. There are many unique factors that influence your mental health during this stage of development, and understanding these aspects is a crucial first step to improving your well-being.

This first chapter introduces several of the key topics that will be discussed in this book, and it aims to explain why this time of your life is so challenging and confusing. It begins by looking at some basic facts related to teen mental health, including the most common disorders and symptoms. It will then explore the different biological, social, and emotional stressors that you might face as a teenager. Finally, this discussion will extend to unique features of today's world: How ever-changing technology, social media, and a once-in-a-lifetime pandemic have created unprecedented challenges for your generation.

It's Not Just You

Mental health is all about maximizing the different kinds of well-being. Having good mental health means feeling healthy and happy from an emotional and psychological perspective. But this state of wellness can be impacted by a range of other factors, including your physical health and social relationships. Moreover, mental health is not only about being happy—it is also about stability, consistency, and resilience.

When you have good mental health, you have a clear idea of who you are and your place in the world. You have an insightful understanding of yourself and your behavior, and you can regulate your own thoughts and emotions. Good mental health means consistency of character—you can hold on to your values and identity and maintain a positive outlook regardless of external circumstances.

Above all else, being mentally well enables you to face life's ups and downs with resilience. You are inevitably going to encounter difficult situations and experience uncomfortable emotions: Being able to work through these challenges without losing your sense of self is a sign of good mental health.

One in Seven

Mental health is more than just the absence of mental illness, but clinical mental disorders are a hugely influential factor when it comes to your thoughts, emotions, and behaviors.

Mental illness can negatively affect your daily routines around eating and sleeping, and can cause you to lose interest in the things that used to make you happy. Other common signs of poor mental health are withdrawing from others and struggling to find motivation to get through the day. Obsessive thoughts, constant anxiety, and feeling low and sad all the time are also good indicators of being mentally unwell. It can be difficult to open up and talk about these things, so many teens also develop negative coping strategies to deal with what's going on in their heads.

If you are experiencing any of these signs or symptoms, you are not alone. It is estimated that 14% of all young people between the ages of 10 and 19 struggle with a mental health condition (World Health Organization, 2021). This means one in every seven adolescents globally, and many of these teens go undiagnosed and untreated.

The most common mental health conditions among adolescents are emotional disorders like anxiety and depression. A lot of teens struggle with extraordinary mood swings and excessive fear and worry. This is also the most likely age at which we see the emergence of behavioral and neurodevelopmental conditions, such as attention deficit hyperactivity disorder (ADHD). Similarly, many eating disorders—like anorexia and bulimia—often begin during the adolescent years.

Moreover, chronic mental illnesses, namely bipolar disorder and schizophrenia, can develop in older teenagers, and these disorders often include psychosis (hallucinations and delusions) as a primary feature. Finally, the adolescent age group has a higher risk of self-harm and suicide than the rest of the population.

Given all this, we have to ask the question of *why*. Why is it that teenagers have such a hard time emotionally and psychologically?

Your Formative Years

You are currently living through a significant period of development. All teens experience a variety of biological and social changes during these years, and many different factors can contribute to your stress.

This is a time of crucial learning and development for you. It is in your adolescence that you form many of the emotional, physical, and interpersonal habits that will define your well-being. This includes creating routines around sleeping, eating, and exercise, developing skills for emotional coping and problem-solving, and honing social and communication skills.

The challenges you face during these years and how you choose to cope with them will establish patterns for your adulthood. It is important that you set a strong foundation for yourself, and the best way to start doing this is to understand exactly what changes you are experiencing.

Body and Biology

From a biological perspective, adolescence is defined by transition. It is underpinned by physical changes that transform your body and mind, carrying you from childhood into adulthood. Regardless of the age at which you experience puberty, most of your teen years will be a journey of adapting to the changes brought on by this process.

Puberty sets off a range of chemical and hormonal changes in your body, most of which will likely be familiar to you. Hair in new places, sexual maturation, and all different kinds of growth—these are the better-known consequences of puberty. What is less understood is how much these changes can affect your mood, interests, performance, and anxieties. Your bodily development is easier to see, but what's happening inside your head is equally important.

The bottom line is that your brain is developing exponentially faster than it did during childhood. You are cultivating all new intellectual and psychological skills: logical deduction, abstract thinking, creativity, and moral reasoning. You are still learning how best to apply these new ways of thinking, and crucially, your brain is nowhere near done with its changes. It still has miles to go when it comes to your frontal cortex. This is the part of the brain that controls executive function and decision-making. So (unfortunately), there is some biological truth to the claim that teens are naturally impulsive, egocentric, and driven by poor judgment.

This isn't a critique or something to worry about, but it is good to be aware of your own limitations. It might not feel like it, but there is still a lot of growing to be done in your head. The frontal cortex doesn't finish developing until your mid-20s, so it is entirely normal to struggle with planning, prioritizing, and seeing the bigger picture. Your brain is literally not yet capable of processing all that there is to comprehend about yourself and the world.

It can be unsettling to feel like you have a narrow or myopic view of life, but this is just the stage that you are in. As you grow, age, and learn, your psychological field of vision will widen. You will be able to take it all in and find your place. Try to remember this if you start to feel ungrounded or lost during these years—your time is coming, and you should be patient with yourself.

Social Struggles

Adolescents are also confronted with a range of new social and interpersonal challenges. Teenagers face a lot of pressure to conform and fit in with their peers. Friendships are more complicated than they were on your childhood playground, and you will naturally start to be more concerned about maintaining relationships and being excluded. Moreover, you may or may not begin to experience an interest in love, romance, and sex—all of which present unique challenges to navigate on top of everything else you are trying to cope with.

It is also common for teenagers to develop difficult relationships with their parents, caregivers, and other family members. Your struggle for independence and agency can be met with either too much or too little support from your loved ones, and often, the foundations of these relationships have to undergo significant change.

Other factors of your home life, like the quality of your living conditions, your access to support services, and your family's socio-economic status, can have huge impacts on your development and socialization. It is not that these factors didn't exist before your teen years—you are now simply more aware of them and their implications for your life and future.

Similarly, a lot of teenagers start to experience increasing stress when it comes to their education. Learning difficulties can emerge, and results and achievements are more important than ever before. The pressures seem endless: keeping up with your classmates, getting good grades, ensuring admission to university or college, performing in your cultural activities, succeeding on the sports' field, and padding your CV with extracurriculars. Rest becomes a foreign concept, and anxiety is the new normal.

Emotional Crisis

Lastly, so much about adolescence can be painful and uncomfortable because this time marks the beginning of emotional and moral regulation. You are becoming more aware of your feelings and developing a sense of self. Your self-esteem and self-confidence are in a fragile state, and your level of independence and capability can be impacted by a variety of factors and events.

Teenagers have to do a lot of hard work to explore their identity and find their character. There is so much pressure to figure out who you are and what you want. You are forced to start thinking more deeply about your values and beliefs. You have to look at yourself and those around you and start to form an opinion on complex topics—religion, spirituality, death, empathy, the future, love, and so much more.

You are exposed to more of the world than you had to deal with as a child. As a result, you are becoming increasingly aware of societal norms and expectations. On one hand, this gives you a much better sense of your place in the world, but the flip side of this coin is your introduction to harsh realities like discrimination, racism, sexism, homophobia, transphobia, abuse, bullying, harassment, and violence.

Moreover, the "hot cognition" of your teen years, driven by your underdeveloped frontal cortex, can push you to risky behavior. Experimentation is normal during adolescence, but the emotional challenges of this time can be overwhelming. Coping mechanisms, like substance abuse, unsafe sexual activity, violence, and self-harm, can emerge as ways of processing difficult feelings and thoughts. There is often so much shame and stigma attached to these behaviors that young people are reluctant to ask for help.

Today's Generation

There is no doubt that you have heard this before, but your generation is special. Growing up with social media and the fast pace of technological advancement is unprecedented. No other generation has had to experience their formative years alongside such drastic and ongoing external change. Everything about being a teenager is uncertain and often unstable, and the need to constantly adapt to the outside world places additional pressure on young people today.

Everyone is overexposed to too much of the world's conflict as a result of living online and the global media. There is endless pressure to stay informed and be proactive about war, climate change, discrimination, inequality, and your generation is being drawn into these discussions earlier, sooner, and faster than ever before.

As with anything, there are pros and cons to social media and technology, but what is most significant is that we do not actually know exactly what the end result will be. It can feel a bit like a global experiment, and teens are already experiencing enough challenges.

Once in a Lifetime

The consequences of the COVID-19 pandemic are similarly uncertain and just as important when exploring factors that are shaping your generation. The pandemic was a once-in-a-lifetime experience that affected everyone differently, but young people bore much of its brunt.

School closures caused extraordinary stress, and many students struggled to adapt to online, self-taught, or hybrid learning. For months, there was limited opportunity for social, sporting, and cultural engagement and restricted access to essential support networks and services.

Even though the pandemic is over, many consequences are ongoing and irreversible. You have missed out on key experiences and milestones, and have had your routine, relationships, and learning disrupted. Much of the damage to your physical, social, and educational outcomes is already done, and many young people are still struggling to get back on track.

Mental Health Matters

More and more teens today are reporting mental health challenges. In a survey conducted by the Centers for Disease Control and Prevention (2020), 42% of U.S. students stated that they felt sad and hopeless a lot of the time, and 29% characterized their mental health as poor.

More than one-fifth of these teens had experienced suicidal thoughts, and one in every ten students had attempted suicide. The groups of young people who reported struggling the most with their mental health were women, racial and ethnic minorities, and members of the LGBTQIA+ community.

Now more than ever, it is vital to value your mental health. It can have knock-on effects for so many different areas in your life, and the sooner you develop healthy strategies for coping and resilience, the happier and more stable you will feel. Despite the challenges that come with this stage of development, you are capable of growing, learning, and adapting. As you work to find and understand yourself during these years, you can also establish a good foundation for your mental health.

CHAPTER 2

All About Anxiety

The first mental health challenge that we are going to explore in this book is anxiety. Anxiety—and its associated disorders—are common among teenagers. As this chapter will explain, it is often concerns over perception and performance that underpin these difficult thoughts and feelings.

To help you better understand what might be going on in your head, we start by looking at the different signs, symptoms, and types of anxiety. This chapter then examines the origin and causes of these feelings, and discusses two of the most common anxiety disorders experienced during adolescence: social anxiety and generalized anxiety disorder. Finally, it concludes by highlighting the role of pressure in causing anxiety in young people—perfectionism is a significant factor to consider when delving into the roots of this mental health struggle.

Busy Head

Anxiety is one of the most common emotional challenges experienced by teenagers. Feelings of fear, worry, nervousness, confusion, and apprehension can all increase as you get older because more and more is being expected of you every day. Additionally, the unique factors of your generation's upbringing—social media, evolving technology, increasing connectedness, and the pandemic—are all associated with a rise in anxiety disorders among young people.

Anxiety is all about fear, and what we are afraid of changes as we grow. Being anxious as a child can include things like being afraid of the dark or thinking that there are monsters hiding under your bed. While this may seem silly to you now, these fears make sense to a younger person because they don't have the context or experience to know any differently. Simply put: Anxiety is an attempt to cope with the unknown.

As a teenager, this can take on a different meaning as your perception of the world and your place in it changes. Your perspective widens, and your focus can shift from external worries (food, comfort, basic needs) to internal concerns and obsessions (weight, achievements, the future, relationships, beliefs, self-esteem). Suddenly, there is so much more going on in your head, and regulating all that information can be challenging.

Signs and Symptoms

Anxiety can feel differently for everyone. Symptoms vary in intensity given an individual's specific triggers and levels of sensitivity, but there are some common signs to look out for.

Feeling constantly panicked, nervous, worried, or apprehensive is a solid indicator that you have anxiety. It is also common to experience obsessive thoughts and excessive fears around ordinary tasks. Anxiety can cause irritability, lashing out, and trouble concentrating or sleeping. It can make you feel agitated, uncomfortable, tense, and self-conscious. Physical symptoms of anxiety can include a racing heart, sweats and chills, hyperventilated breathing, and chest pain.

If you struggle with anxiety, you might start to change your behavior by avoiding places, people, or situations that upset or trigger you. Moreover, you may seek repeated reassurance from others, and might come to depend on external validation and comfort. Anxiety can also manifest in recurring physical ailments, such as frequent headaches or stomachaches. Ultimately, if severe and unmanaged, your worries and fears can make it difficult to stick to your routine and to get through the responsibilities of each day.

Adolescent Anxiety

A particularly common consequence of anxiety in teenagers is something called "school refusal." This refers to a young person's resistance, reluctance, and fear around attending school. It is usually a sign that they are experiencing anxiety driven by performance or socializing, not that they are afraid of school or learning in and of itself.

Similarly, many teens suffer from panic and anxiety attacks, which are significant indicators of a possible underlying anxiety disorder. These intense moments of panic and fear bring on a range of emotional, cognitive, and physical symptoms.

Finally, another response to anxiety that is often seen in adolescents is the emergence of negative coping strategies in an attempt to deal with discomfort. These can range from the recreational use of alcohol and drugs—most common, marijuana—to the abuse of these substances, as well as self-harm behaviors.

Stressing Out

So, what exactly is anxiety? Where does it come from, and why do we experience it?

Anxiety has an evolutionary origin. As humans, we are biologically programmed to sense danger or stress. Once our brains perceive a threat, our bodies set off physical and cognitive processes to help us defend ourselves. This is the fight, flight, or freeze response, and it is physiologically natural and psychologically normal. Everyone experiences some level of worry, fear, or anxiety, and some people just have more sensitive and hyperactive systems than others.

Whether it is due to genetics, upbringing, or a traumatic experience, it may simply be the case that your body and mind are in a heightened state of awareness and response. This can become problematic and disordered if it begins to interfere with your functioning and well-being. It is at this point that you should consider actively dealing with your fear and worry.

Disorders and Triggers

As with its symptoms, the triggers of anxiety can be individual and unique. Everyone is afraid of different things, and each person has had their own life experiences, which form their fears.

To figure out what kind of anxiety you might be struggling with, let's take a look at two of the most common anxiety disorders that emerge in adolescence.

Social Anxiety Disorder

Social anxiety disorder is a mental health condition that often begins during the teen years, and it is driven by a concern over how you are being perceived in social situations. You may worry excessively and obsessively about saying or doing something embarrassing in public or in front of others. You might be convinced that people will laugh at and mock you, and you may be afraid of being isolated and ostracized.

If you struggle with social anxiety, you are likely often very uncomfortable and tense in social situations, and you find interpersonal interactions and relationships challenging. You are either overly emotional or too restrained when dealing with others, and you just feel like none of this *socializing stuff* comes naturally to you.

Generalized Anxiety Disorder

Generalized anxiety disorder is characterized by excessive and persistent worry. The feelings and fear underpinning this condition are much more general and nonspecific than other kinds of anxiety disorders.

If you struggle with generalized anxiety, you will find that you always feel nervous, like something bad is going to happen, but you can't pinpoint exactly what is bothering you. You have a sense of impending doom, and every action you take is weighed down with implication and consequence because *you just never know what could happen.*

This kind of free-floating unease and discomfort doesn't usually have a specific trigger, but it can cause you to struggle with everyday activities and ordinary tasks. Because you don't have an actual target for your anxiety, you tend to attach these feelings to whatever difficulties or challenges you face on any given day.

The trouble with this is that it means almost anything can trigger your panic. You are afraid of things that everyone else seems to have no trouble with, and the prospect of any kind of uncertainty is terrifying.

Pressure and Perception

The root of a lot of anxiety in young people is pressure—both externally applied and self-imposed.

As a teenager, you are relatively inexperienced and lacking in context about the world and your place in it. You may feel lost and confused, and people your age are often impressionable and vulnerable to influence. The need to fit in is normal. Everyone wants to feel safe and grounded, and having a way to describe and identify yourself is particularly comforting as a young person. It is when the pressure to be, look, and act in a certain way starts to overwhelm you that your anxiety around perception can become debilitating.

There are many external factors that try to force you to think and act in a certain way. Your family and parents might have specific expectations of you related to your social relationships, academic and sporting achievements, or religious and cultural beliefs.

It is also easy to get swept up in what your peers are doing. Teens worry a lot about what their friends will think, whether or not they will be liked, and how they will be perceived by others. No one wants to be too different, and society's norms can be irresistible.

Social media, in particular, creates a vast array of reasons for self-consciousness, and young people start to worry about things that never concerned them before—money, class, lifestyle, popularity, and body image. These factors promote and instill a hypervigilance about how you present yourself to the world. Reality can become a subjective and manipulative experience, and how you perform can seem more important than how you really feel.

Perfectionism

In the face of these new anxieties, many teens fall into the trap of perfectionism.

Perfectionism is a coping strategy for a range of difficult feelings and uncomfortable experiences. It allows you to channel all of your worry and fear toward performance and achievement. You focus your anxiety on doing well academically or succeeding in competition. You become consumed by potential and performance, and you no longer have to face up to the bigger questions that scare you—who are you, what do you want, are you good enough, and what does it all mean?

Perfectionism allows you to have a measurable scale and quantifiable set of standards for yourself. You can spend all your time worrying about doing well in school, getting into an elite university, being the best player on the team, or having the most friends. While this provides a worthy distraction, the trouble is that you become obsessed with doing the best rather than *your* best. Moreover, you begin to rely on external achievement and praise from others as your validation, and in this way, you neglect the development of your own personality and sense of self.

Perfectionism is an incredibly unstable and fragile way to measure your self-worth. You may develop an extraordinary work ethic, but this level of intensity is unsustainable. Eventually, you will burn out, lose interest, and even overcorrect by giving up on or quitting what you thought you loved.

Once the top marks and trophies are gone or meaningless, the cracks in your perception of yourself will begin to show. You will have no other way of determining if you are a good enough person, and the self-doubt and anxiety that follows can do real damage.

Costly Consequences

As with many mental health challenges, you might still be able to function well despite your anxiety and distress. But this will be at the cost of your well-being and mental health.

Whatever coping mechanism you are relying on to deal with your anxiety is creating enduring patterns of dependence that you will carry with you into adulthood. These unhealthy strategies can be dangerous and hard to untangle from your core self. Moreover, untreated anxiety can lead to depression, isolation, and other mental health challenges.

The most important takeaway message for this chapter is that you don't have to feel this way. You are deserving of help and peace of mind, and there are different ways to manage and overcome anxiety. Therapy can change your thinking patterns and outlook, and medication can help to minimize your fear.

Ultimately, you also need to learn to find value in who you are, not in what you can do or how others see you. This will ensure that you are not so susceptible to external challenges and changes—your strength will come from within.

CHAPTER 3

Depression, Mood Swings, and Burnout

Depression is another condition that is regularly experienced by adolescents. The symptoms and consequences of this mood disorder can be isolating and debilitating, but you do not have to struggle alone. Many people—adults included—experience bouts of depression throughout their lives, and there are different treatment options to help get you out of a dark place.

This chapter explores depression in more detail so that you can better understand what you might be going through. It highlights how this mental health disorder differs from ordinary mood swings, and examines the potential symptoms and causes of clinical depression. Additionally, this chapter covers other conditions and factors that could be affecting your mood, including mania, hypomania, and burnout.

The most important thing to remember about this topic is that depression is not a sign of weakness. You have not done anything wrong, and there is no shame in needing and asking for help.

When You're Not Just Moody

As a teenager, you have probably been told countless times that you should stop being *so moody*.

The perception that adolescents are always grumpy, irritable, and filled with angst is a common one. It does have some foundational truth because there are a lot of normal mood changes during this stage of development. Remember that your brain is still growing and your emotional and moral regulation has only just begun. Your body is buzzing with hormones, and you're facing all new challenges from every direction. In other words, a little bit of mood instability is to be expected.

But moodiness is not the same as depression. Being a teenager can be difficult, but you shouldn't constantly feel sad, lost, and hopeless. If it seems like your life has become unmanageably dark and overwhelmingly gloomy, then you're likely struggling with more than just the everyday highs and lows of adolescence.

Defining Depression

Depression is a type of clinical mood disorder. It is a recognized mental health condition, and it is characterized by a range of symptoms that can vary in intensity. Everyone's experience of depression can be unique, and this condition is about much more than just feeling blue.

Depression is like living with a dark cloud hanging over your head. It turns the world to gray, and leaves you feeling empty and restless. You can't see how things could get better, and you don't really remember what it was like to feel any lighter. You are weighed down by emotional and physical exhaustion, and it can feel like someone has snuffed out every light inside of you. Everything feels like it is moving in slow motion, like you are constantly wading through thick quicksand. You have the urge to lie in bed all day and stare at the walls.

You feel sad and anxious a lot of the time, but you also feel numb and bored. Nothing interests you anymore—you want to care about things and people, but you just can't. You have no motivation or concentration, and you can't bear to think about the future. Life seems long, pointless, and purposeless. You don't know how to make yourself feel better, and you don't have the energy to try anyway. Simply eating, sleeping, and getting through the day leaves you breathless. Depression can feel like drowning, with no shoreline or lifeguard in sight.

Despite being desensitized, you also find yourself feeling overly emotional. You are easily irritated and frustrated, and you fixate on your mistakes. Depression and its side effects can cause intense guilt and self-hate. You alternate between tearfulness and apathy, and in your worst moments, you feel overwhelming panic set in: *What if this never goes away? What if I feel like this forever?*

Finding a Cause

If you are struggling with some of these thoughts and feelings, you could meet the diagnostic criteria for depression. Specifically, you need to be experiencing several of the clinical symptoms of this condition every day for at least two weeks.

Feeling this low all of the time is not normal, and untreated depression can seep into every aspect of your life. It affects all areas of well-being. You withdraw from others, struggle with school, and fight with your parents and friends. Your emotional state is in chaos, and your physical health declines. It is also possible that you start to have thoughts of self-harm and suicide, although this is not a prerequisite for depression. Moreover, your symptoms can come and go or even change over time.

The causes of this mental health condition are similarly unique, and identifying what might be fueling your distress can help you to better understand why you feel this way.

Life

Depression can be triggered by a range of stressful life events. For teens, this can include any of the challenges we have discussed so far and many more: difficult family life, pressure to conform, academic stress, loneliness, changes to your body, anxiety, identity crises, and relationship conflict.

It is also important to remember that stress can be sneaky. You might not feel overwhelmed by your life, but a lot of this pressure may be internalized and subconscious. Being stressed, busy, and anxious could be a normalized state for you, and even though you are used to it, your mind and body may be struggling to keep up.

Chemistry

Depression is also often genetic. It can be the result of a family history of mental health struggles, and you may have inherited biology that is predisposed to this condition.

In other words, depression can have a physical cause, and this is often the easiest way to come to terms with what is happening in your head. The brain is made up of chemical messengers called neurotransmitters that control how you think, feel, and act. When the signal senders that monitor your mood, sleep, attention, motivation, and pleasure are disrupted, imbalanced, or in short supply, you can start to develop symptoms of depression. Dopamine and serotonin are the primary culprits in this process, which is why antidepressant medication often targets the production and uptake of these neurotransmitters.

Adolescent onset of this kind of depression is common given the various other triggers teens face during this time. It can be the case that your depression is being driven by a combination of factors—a genetic predisposition to chemical imbalance and the stress of teenage life. Your brain is simply overwhelmed, and it hasn't figured out how to make you happy in a consistent way.

Mania and Other Moods

Speaking of consistency, there are other types of mood disorders that you could be struggling with. Remember that it is normal to have mood swings as a teenager, but cycling up and down on a regular basis and in an extreme way could be a sign of clinical mood instability.

Mania

Mania is a state of extraordinary energy. It is a mental health condition in which a person experiences huge amounts of physical and emotional motivation. They feel unusually happy and high on life itself, and they are extremely intense, confident, and focused.

Being in a manic state can feel good, euphoric even, but it also has its downsides. People in the midst of an episode are often impulsive and poor decision-makers. They engage in risky behavior without thinking through the consequences of their actions. Fast speech, racing thoughts, and insomnia are also common symptoms and side effects of mania, which can cause a lot of distress and discomfort.

Mania is not as common in teenagers as depression, but when it does manifest, it often looks more like irritability and restlessness than euphoria. It can be frustrating to have all this energy and drive and not know what to do with it. Your thoughts are spinning around so fast in your head that you can't keep up. You feel untethered, like you could just float away. You are happy, but it doesn't feel sustainable or stable, and you have a feeling that it's going to all come crashing down.

Bipolar Disorder

Manic episodes swing you up, then depression brings you back down—again and again, on and on. This type of mood instability is characteristic of bipolar disorder, and it can be an exhausting and uncertain way to live.

Bipolar disorder is a mental health condition that usually emerges during the late teen and young adult years. It is a mood disorder involving extreme highs and lows, and someone with bipolar disorder will struggle with depression but also experience manic episodes. The degree of intensity of these mood swings will narrow down a bipolar disorder diagnosis.

It is more common to experience hypomania than true mania. This is a slightly less intense condition, a milder form of mania, that lasts for shorter stretches. Hypomania can feel like a constant, low hum of pressure, anxiety, irritability, and restless energy.

Coupled with repeated and cycling depressive episodes, you can get a diagnosis of bipolar II disorder.

The difference between bipolar I and bipolar II disorder is the occurrence of a psychotic break. If a manic state is truly intense and lengthy enough, it can escalate to psychosis. This is a mental health condition characterized by delusions and hallucinations, and while it can make the highs higher, it brings an even lower depression in the aftermath.

Burnout

Instead of indicating a clinical mental illness, the symptoms of depression and other mood disorders can be a sign of burnout.

Burnout is exhaustion. It is a state of being overwhelmed by your commitments, relationships, and responsibilities, and it can feel like chronic tiredness—physical, emotional, and existential. Burnout is a sign that life has become too much. You have been moving too fast, trying too hard, and doing too many things for too long, and you can't keep up anymore.

Remember: Stress is sneaky. If you don't give yourself a chance to rest, your body and mind are eventually going to force you to take a break. This is often the most difficult part of burnout—you run out of fumes, even when you don't want to. This can happen at the most inopportune time, and is so challenging to accept because it was not your choice. If you had it your way, you would carry on forever—full speed ahead with friends, school, sports, relationships, social media, drama, college admission, and extracurriculars.

But this is not sustainable, and when you reach the end of your rope, the burnout can be as debilitating as chronic depression. Many of the symptoms overlap, and burnout can bring the same sense of hopelessness, futility, and exhaustion.

Trying Hard Enough

Many people have a distorted view of depression, especially when they don't understand exactly what is happening to them and why. They think that depression is something that they can fix if only they could *just get it together*.

But depression cannot be willed away. There is either a chemical imbalance in your brain, unmanageable external circumstances, or a combination of factors driving your thoughts and feelings. Something has to give or change, and there are treatments that can get you through a depressive episode. So, why not get help?

Ultimately, coping with depression isn't about trying hard enough, being good enough, or being stronger because you are not a bad person for struggling in this way. Mental illness is not a sign of personal weakness, so there is no need to be ashamed of how you are feeling.

You haven't done anything wrong, and the flip side of that coin is that you deserve to get help. You don't have to struggle, suffer, and strive all on your own, and you shouldn't waste valuable healing time by believing that you aren't worthy of happiness.

CHAPTER 4

Neurodiversity

As we saw in the previous chapter, someone struggling with depression may have different brain chemistry compared to other people. This is an important theme when it comes to understanding mental health challenges—not everyone's brain works in the same way. In fact, the term neurodiversity has been coined as a way of acknowledging cognitive and developmental individuality.

This chapter explores the concept of neurodiversity as another way of helping you to understand why you might feel, think, and act differently to your peers. It defines this term in more detail, and highlights the various conditions that are recognized under its umbrella. Finally, this chapter examines the most common form of neurodiversity among adolescents: ADHD.

Not Neurotypical

Mental health has a lot to do with how your brain works, and a more contemporary way of recognizing unique challenges and differences is by acknowledging neurodiversity. You don't have to be diagnosed with a formal mental illness, like anxiety or depression, to feel like your mind is different.

Neurodiversity is an umbrella term used to describe any kind of atypical cognitive functioning. Someone who develops and learns differently to the majority of the population will have a different set of strengths and weaknesses. They will face their own emotional and social challenges, and will succeed in ways that other people cannot. And, that is the crux of it all—neurodiversity is about describing differences and not deficits.

No Such Thing as Normal

The advantage of this term is that it allows us to avoid labels like normal and abnormal. Normal implies that there is a right and wrong way to be. It leads people to believe that being different is the same as being bad, weak, and inferior. The consequences of this can be the same as with any form of preconceived prejudice or ignorance—discrimination, exclusion, and ostracization.

It is much more inclusive and helpful to simply accept that everyone is unique. What may seem typical, based on a majority or ongoing pattern, does not have to apply to each person. We don't have to use any set of standards to gatekeep our society. There is, in fact, no single definition of how the brain and body work, and moving away from this mainstream understanding opens us up to a variety of possibilities.

It is also incredibly useful to recognize the distinctive aspects of an atypical person's experience. Because their brain is wired differently, they will have thought processes, feelings, and behaviors that stand out from the crowd. A neurodiverse person's development will take place at a unique pace, and they will hit the typical milestones in their own way and time. It is important to nurture and value what makes us all different and to do our best as a society to accommodate diversity and minorities.

Self-Identification

Being neurodiverse is generally not something about yourself that you can change. It is an innate part of your biology, brain development, and overall functioning. Even if you only find out during your teen or young adult years that you might fall under this umbrella, it does not mean that you weren't this way all along.

Genetics play a strong role in determining neurodiversity, and you can inherit the genes for certain conditions that make up this classification. The environment and experiences of your upbringing are also crucially important as causal factors for neurodiversity. Many of the features of an atypical person's functioning and processing are the result of unique developmental and learning differences.

To be included under the banner of neurodiversity, you can be formally diagnosed with one of the recognized conditions. You can also self-identify as part of this group if you relate to the signs, symptoms, and experiences of an atypical person. Labels can be as meaningful as you want them to be. What is more important is the self-acceptance that goes along with describing yourself as neurodiverse.

Neurodiversity is not a problem or issue in and of itself. Remember: There is no right or wrong, normal or abnormal, when it comes to how your brain works. Moreover, as you will see below, not all presentations of neurodiversity are considered medical conditions, mental illnesses, or disabilities that need constant care and management. The fundamental takeaway about acknowledging your own neurodiversity is the importance of understanding yourself. You need to know who you are, where you struggle and thrive, and how you can best accommodate yourself in more neurotypical settings.

The Umbrella

Since we have already discussed several of them in detail, we can start by putting mental illnesses under the umbrella of neurodiversity. This includes mental health disorders like anxiety, depression, and bipolar disorder, as well as others such as obsessive-compulsive disorder.

As mentioned, neurodiversity also encompasses several recognized medical conditions. These include Down syndrome, autism spectrum disorder, and Tourette's syndrome. Neurodiversity also describes a range of learning, developmental, and processing conditions, including dyslexia, dyspraxia (coordination disorder), and intellectual disabilities. Finally, neurodiversity can be triggered by brain trauma, stroke, or other illnesses like dementia.

Attention and Activity

Another notable condition that falls into the category of neurodiversity is ADHD. ADHD is a neurodevelopmental disorder that can start showing its first signs in children and young teenagers. Unfortunately, ADHD is regularly unrecognized and undiagnosed, and its symptoms and consequences are easily confused with anxiety, depression, and other mental health and behavioral challenges.

As its name suggests, ADHD is a condition characterized by inattention and hyperactivity. It is normal for both children and adolescents to struggle with consistency in these areas, but ADHD is about more than just having too much energy and too little focus.

There is a common misperception that young people with ADHD are being difficult on purpose. They are labeled as *handfuls* and *troublemakers*, and everyone accepts that they like to misbehave or rebel. Teens with ADHD can be disruptive in class, and they battle to sit still for a full lesson. They are often in trouble with their teachers and parents, and even though this behavior starts at a very young age, they are aware of their differences. They know that they stand out from their peers, which can be incredibly isolating, and they see how certain things come more easily to their classmates or friends.

Ultimately, untreated and unmanaged ADHD can detrimentally interfere with your development, functioning, learning, and well-being. If you're not sure if you meet the criteria for a diagnosis, take a look at the possible symptoms below.

Difficulties of Neurodiversity

ADHD has two categories of symptoms and consequences: Those related to the inattention side of the equation, and those that are driven by hyperactivity.

When it comes to receiving a diagnosis, this division will be relevant as you can present as either predominantly inattentive or primarily hyperactive. Younger adolescents tend toward hyperactivity while older teens manifest more often as inattentive. Complicating matters is the possibility of experiencing a combination of these symptoms, and this overlap is actually the most common form of ADHD.

Focus

The inattention part of ADHD refers to an inability to focus. If you have this form of ADHD, you can struggle with concentration and motivation. It can be difficult for you to follow a conversation, and you may spend a lot of time drifting in and out of reality. Daydreaming is a favorite pastime, but it can get you in trouble when you have to pay attention.

Your inattentive nature can also mean that you battle to take direction and initiative, and you aren't great at working independently or quietly. You are easily distracted by things you find more interesting, and you can't stay focused on one thing for too long without getting fidgety and restless. Organizing and planning are not your strengths, and you prefer spontaneity, excitement, and embarking on something new.

Impulse

The hyperactivity side of ADHD can manifest in similar ways, but it also has its own set of symptoms. Someone who is predominantly hyperactive is in constant motion. You are always on the go, busy with one thing or another, and moving from this place to the next. This behavior can mimic mania, and there is a similar element of impulsivity involved.

This drives your desire for new and exciting experiences, but it also leads to an intense emotionality. You may find it hard to compromise, read social cues, and understand someone else's perspective. You can get fixated on a particular activity or way of doing things, and might find yourself trapped in egocentric and rigid ways of thinking.

Diagnosis

All of these difficulties can converge and cause problems in various areas of your life.

ADHD can hinder your academic performance in neurotypical institutions and settings. You struggle with deadlines, prioritizing, and procrastinating, but you know you would do so much better if you could just do things *your way*. Your ADHD can also lead to trouble in your social relationships because you and your peers are functioning on different levels and in different ways. You might find yourself interrupting them when they're talking and forgetting details that are important to them. Finally, your impulsivity can drive you to take unnecessary risks, which can create its own set of problems.

There are a lot of comorbidities among ADHD and other mental health challenges—primarily, depression and anxiety. Being different also places a huge strain on your self-esteem, and constantly having to adapt to mainstream, neurotypical ways of doing things can be exhausting and discouraging.

To end on a positive note, there is medication available that can help you deal with the more challenging aspects of your ADHD, like concentration and focus. Moreover, different kinds of therapy can teach you coping skills for social and academic situations.

In other words, there are ways to adapt to and thrive in your current environment. Many features of ADHD can persist into your adulthood, and neurodiversity will always be an innate part of your biology. Ultimately, learning to understand, accept, and manage yourself early on is vitally important.

CHAPTER 5

Identity: Who Am I?

It is also possible that the challenges you face in your teen years are not necessarily diagnosable mental illnesses or conditions. You can struggle with all kinds of questions and uncertainty that detrimentally affect your mental health, and this chapter will explore one of the more common pain points for adolescents.

Knowing who you are and what you want out of life can be extremely difficult. Identity formation is an ongoing learning process that involves understanding your personality and coming to terms with your place in the world.

This chapter aims to help you answer the question of who you are. It examines the concept of identity and why you should start exploring your potential. It then discusses personality in more detail by highlighting different personality theories, traits, and disorders. Finally, this chapter looks at what it means to have an identity or existential crises—uncertainty and change can be terrifying, but in the end, you have to become more comfortable with the unknown.

Trying It On

It is very common for young people to try out different personas and to put on different characters. This is an essential part of experimentation, and it helps teens to form a stronger sense of themselves. Trying on personas can include things like changing your hobbies and extracurriculars very often, taking up with a new friend group on a regular basis, and going through different character phases—being funny and loud, quiet and thoughtful, full of energy and social, or spending more time alone.

In other words, it is entirely normal to have a certain level of inconsistency of character during your teen years. It can cause confusion—for you and your loved ones—but it is a natural part of growing up. It can also be fun and exciting to figure out who you are and what you like best. Crucially, as you experiment, you will be able to gather more information about yourself and the world, and all of this experience is channeled toward your identity formation.

An Amalgamation

So, what is identity?

Identity is an amalgamation of all the various factors that make you who you are: experiences, relationships, values, decisions, roles, memories, external characteristics, and innate traits. One way of thinking about identity is to visualize different puzzle pieces fitting together or to picture blocks being stacked on top of one another.

The foundation or center pieces of your identity will be the characteristics you were born with and the traits you cannot change. This includes your genetics, family history, race, sex, sexual orientation, physical appearance, and so on. All of these factors will shape how you think, feel, and behave in some way or another.

Your next set of puzzle pieces or building blocks are derived from the external environment. As you live in the world, your experiences and memories will start to shape who you are. This is the latter part of the nature versus nurture debate, and it covers significant elements that can affect your character: upbringing, parenting styles, childhood environment, quality of home life, exposure to trauma, socio-economic status, socialization, education, and relationships. Life events and circumstances all add to your tapestry of identity, and as you take on different roles—child, sibling, friend, student—you will discover new ways of defining yourself.

The final part of your identity is more subjective and within your own control. You will make countless choices over your lifetime. Some can be life altering while others turn out to be insignificant, but they all play a part in cultivating your character. What you choose to believe and value are also important aspects of this category. Who you want to be, how you express yourself, and what you want to do with your life—these are all defining decisions that can help answer the question of identity.

Identity Distress

This process of finding yourself can seem overwhelming, but a lot of it takes place subconsciously and under the surface level. The only really important role that you need to play is making sure you know who you are.

A person can experience extreme distress when a core aspect of their identity is not adequately nurtured or expressed. If you neglect, ignore, or suppress a key part of yourself, you will never realize your full potential or maximize your well-being.

Your mental health is also heavily dependent on congruence between who you are and what you do. What this means is that you need to make sure that your behavior and goals match up with your core beliefs, values, and traits. You can't force yourself to be something you are not, and trying to mold your identity according to external expectations will only lead to stress and low self-esteem.

To avoid these two pitfalls of identity formation, you need to start by exploring your innate traits and potential. Figuring out who you really are is the first step to making choices that express and align with your identity.

Defining Personality

Personality is one the foundational building blocks of your identity, so this is the perfect place to start with your journey of self-discovery.

Personality refers to the innate and inherent characteristics and patterns that drive your thoughts, feelings, and behavior. Much of your personality is derived from your genetics and biology, but certain traits can be influenced by the external circumstances of your childhood upbringing.

Your personality generally only solidifies once you reach early adulthood, but then, these traits are considered fairly stable throughout the rest of your life. Once again, adolescence is a time of transition, and it is crucial that you get comfortable with your developing personality.

Types and Traits

There are many different theories of personality, and if you've ever taken an aptitude test, you will likely be familiar with some of them.

The Big Five

One mainstream understanding is the Big Five personality theory. This theory states that everyone has a certain amount or level of five essential personality traits: openness, extroversion, agreeableness, conscientiousness, and emotional stability.

Like most schools of thought, the Big Five theory argues that each of these traits exists on a spectrum and a person can range from one extreme to the other. For example, you could be closer to one end of the extroversion scale, which means you get your energy from social and outgoing behavior. Or, you might tip toward the other side—introverts are more reserved, and they feel comfortable spending time alone.

The agreeableness spectrum is a scale of altruism. It reflects your level of kindness, empathy, trustworthiness, and compassion in relation to others. Openness measures your response toward, and feelings around, change and new experiences. It also includes elements like creativity and curiosity. Conscientiousness is the same as thoughtfulness and diligence. At one extreme of this spectrum are those who are rigidly hard-working, perfectionistic, and detail-oriented, and at the other, are people who tend to be more impulsive, messy, and disorganized. Finally, emotional stability reflects consistency of mood and your response to stress.

Types A, B, C, and D

This is just one understanding, and there are several others. For instance, you may have heard someone describe themselves as a type A person or as having a type B personality. This theory is simply another way of grouping characteristics together.

Type A people are ambitious, competitive, and driven by achievement, while the type B personality is more patient, creative, and easy-going. There is also a type C designation (analytical, logical, and ordered), as well as a type D personality (empathetic, insightful, and reflective).

This categorization is often closely linked to career aptitude, and it is used to determine what kind of work environment a person might be best suited to.

Myers-Briggs

You might also have come across strange looking acronyms like INFJ, ESTP, ISTJ, and so on. These are determined by the popular Myers-Briggs Type Indicator, and each acronym represents a different personality type.

There are 16 possible types, and the letters are derived from your position on four different spectrums of personality traits: introversion versus extroversion, sensing versus intuition, thinking versus feeling, and judging versus perceiving.

This test involves filling out a series of questionnaires about your psychological and social preferences, and the goal is to determine how you make decisions and perceive the world around you.

The Challenge of Personality

If you are curious about your exact personality type, you can always take one of these tests. Many can be done online, with a school guidance counselor, or as part of your career preparation. You can also examine the different characteristics and traits of these groups and decide for yourself where you best fit in.

The most important thing to keep in mind is that these theories are not the be-all and end-all when it comes to your identity. There are other factors that will shape who you are, and you do not have to force yourself into a specific type if you do not want to.

Moreover, there is no right or wrong personality trait to have. None of these characteristics are negative in and of themselves, and they are also usually not things about yourself that you can change. This is the challenge of personality—knowing and accepting yourself as you are.

As mentioned, it is completely normal to feel confused and uncertain at your age. But actively learning to explore and love yourself for who you are is the best way to deal with any insecurity. You will continue with this self-discovery throughout your teenage and young adult years, so it's okay to take it slow at the start.

Personality Disorders

Having said all this, it is still possible to struggle with aspects of your personality. For example, if you are naturally less agreeable, you might find it challenging to see another person's point of view, which can cause problems in your social relationships. Or, your tendency toward the type A personality can lead you to perfectionism and burnout. Each trait has its own strengths and weaknesses, and it is more a case of learning to adapt and grow than trying to change your fundamental nature.

This is most clear when we think about personality disorders. These are a class of mental health conditions characterized by thoughts, feelings, and behaviors that differ substantially from societal norms and expectations. Having a personality disorder can impair your well-being by interfering with your ability to socialize, function independently, maintain relationships, and regulate your emotions.

There are three clusters of clinical personality disorders:

- Cluster A are the conditions that include odd and eccentric features, for example, paranoid personality disorder and schizotypal personality disorder.

- Cluster B is all about the erratic and dramatic, and these conditions include antisocial personality disorder and borderline personality disorder.

- Finally, the conditions characterized by fearful and anxious thoughts and behaviors are grouped in cluster C, and examples of these are avoidant personality disorder and dependent personality disorder.

Like with all mental illnesses, you are not to blame if you struggle with one of these conditions, but since their symptoms and manifestations can be distressing, you should consider seeking help. Treating personality disorders is all about learning management and coping skills. It is about finding better ways to interact with others, and developing new patterns for perceiving yourself and the world around you.

Diagnosis during adolescence is slightly controversial because your personality is still fluid and forming. But if you are worried or struggling, there is no harm in gathering more information and cultivating new skills.

Existential Crisis

On this journey of self-discovery, you are going to be confronted with complex, complicated, and uncomfortable concepts. You may even be riddled with anxiety over really big questions.

Which university will I go to? How will I get a job one day? What job do I even want, and what am I going to do with my life? How will I support myself? Will I be happy? What if I'm not? Do I want to get married? Should I have children and a family? What do I believe in? Is there a god? What happens when we die? What are we all doing here?

Stop for a moment, and take a deep breath. In and out. Everything will be okay.

It is very normal to have these questions and concerns, and everyone worries about these things. You are not alone in trying to figure it all out, and you are definitely not the only one who is overwhelmed by the possibilities. Moreover, this time of your life is a particularly stressful period to be tackling this uncertainty. Your brain is still developing but at a faster rate than ever before. More and more is being asked of you, and your world is only getting bigger. Of course, it's a lot to deal with.

Letting Go

One of the best ways to cope with all of this is to practice acceptance. Uncertainty and change are constants in life, and there are always going to be things that you don't know. This is perfectly okay. You will always have unanswered questions, and much of life will remain a mystery. Everyone—adults included—needs to come to terms with this to some extent.

So, practice letting go of some of this existential dread. Relieve yourself of the pressure to figure it all out right now. Give yourself time—because there is a lot of it—and take things as they come. Deal with the problems and challenges that directly affect you right now. Work out what you can change, what is within your control, and cross each bridge as you reach it. Keep putting one foot in front of the other, and have faith in yourself that you will find your way.

Acceptance is such an important life skill. Being able to acknowledge what you cannot change will bring you peace and relief, and having the strength to change what you can control creates a foundation of confidence. Figuring out the difference between these two takes time and practice, but everyone is capable of this wisdom.

Purpose

Now that you have a much better understanding of yourself, the final step of identity formation is to practically apply this knowledge. This means channeling what you have learned about yourself toward finding a purpose for your life.

Your purpose can be whatever makes you happy. It should be something that fulfills you and allows you to express all the aspects of your identity. It must match up with who you are at the core, and once you've discovered it, you can start exploring different ways to express this purpose.

Keep in mind that identity and personality change over time, so your purpose and potential can transform as well. Everything is a process of ongoing growth. Be kind to yourself as you figure out who you are and what you want.

CHAPTER 6

Gender Versus Sex

To follow on from the previous chapter, there are two aspects of identity that we need to explore in more detail. Gender identity and sexual orientation are important factors that make a person who they are, and uncovering these parts of yourself during adolescence can be a struggle.

Experimentation is normal for teenagers, but it can be confusing. Moreover, young people who identify as queer in some way may need to be prepared to face unique challenges as part of the LGBTQIA+ community.

This chapter begins with a discussion of gender and gender identity. It highlights crucial terms to understand, examines gender dysphoria, and delves into the idea that gender can be fluid in different ways. It then moves on to sexual orientation, and explains the spectrum of sexuality in more detail. Finally, this chapter looks at the LGBTQIA+ community and how members of this group often face extraordinary discrimination and prejudice. It concludes with a note on coming out as a way of fully expressing your identity.

Transcending Gender

Your generation is the most familiar with the distinction between sex and gender. Sex refers to your biological designation at birth, which is based on chromosomes, genes, and genitalia, while gender is how you choose to identify and is driven by your psychological experience and expression of sex.

This distinction is a lot more mainstream and accepted than it has been in the past. It is now more understood that it is possible to have a different identity than the designation you received at birth—it does not make you disordered, sick, or crazy. It can, however, still present a range of social and emotional challenges, as both you and those around you come to terms with your innate disconnect.

Gender Dysphoria

Gender dysphoria is a recognized mental health challenge. It is the term used to describe the physical, emotional, and social distress associated with an incongruence between biological sex and gender identity. When these do not match up, a person is described as transgender. This is in contrast to cisgender, which is the term for someone whose sex assignment and gender identity are the same.

It is usually early on in childhood that a transgender person begins to realize there is something fundamentally different about the way they experience their body and gender role. There is an innate disconnect between what they are being told by society and who they feel like they really are. The world imposes gendered clothes, toys, and games that don't match their identity, and the discomfort and distress they feel can be overwhelming.

Gender dysphoria is then often amplified during puberty when a person's primary and secondary sex organs begin to develop. The physical changes of sexual maturation, as well as the increased exposure to society's gender norms, escalate this feeling of *wrongness*.

Signs and Symptoms

It is also at this point that many of the clinical signs of gender dysphoria emerge. These symptoms include wanting to get rid of your own sex characteristics and organs or to prevent their development. You can experience a desire to have the traits of another gender or to be treated as a member of a different gender. You might start to act like or express yourself as the gender you identify with, which can cause conflict with your family and friends.

People struggle to understand how confusing and distressing it can be to feel like you were born in the wrong body. Having to watch yourself turn into a person you don't recognize is akin to psychological torture. The emotional strain of feeling like it is all out for your control, like you'll never get to be who you really are, is almost too much. You see your friends hit milestones and take on their gender roles with ease and excitement, and you feel lost, left behind, and left out.

Gender dysphoria can manifest as anxiety, depression, and shame. You constantly feel uncomfortable and self-conscious. You can't be confident in how you look or act, and you may even come to hate your body and all that it represents. Something is wrong or missing, and you feel misunderstood in a way that even you can't quite explain.

Fluidity of Gender

There is hope, however, as society becomes more and more accustomed to the idea of gender fluidity. It is now commonly accepted that gender exists on a spectrum, and people are starting to learn that things aren't as black and white—or male and female—as they might have thought.

Gender diversity is the umbrella term being used to capture this nuance. It expresses the idea that there are many different ways to experience gender and that the traditional binary division doesn't come close to representing all the possibilities. For example, a person can even identify as nonbinary. Someone who is nonbinary essentially epitomizes gender diversity because they don't identify with any gender in particular—their concept of gender fluctuates, and they can see themselves as part of one, several, or no genders.

Gender expression is another significant way of encapsulating gender fluidity. It is about how you choose to express and experience gender in an outwardly sense. Your gender expression does not have to match your gender identity, and wanting to express aspects of a different gender is not the same as experiencing gender dysphoria.

In other words, you can be cisgender and identify as female, but choose to wear what is more traditionally men's clothing. You don't relate to society's expectations around womanhood, and you feel more comfortable doing your own thing. Ultimately, gender expression is about challenging societal norms and expectations and finding ways to express the nuance of your preferences.

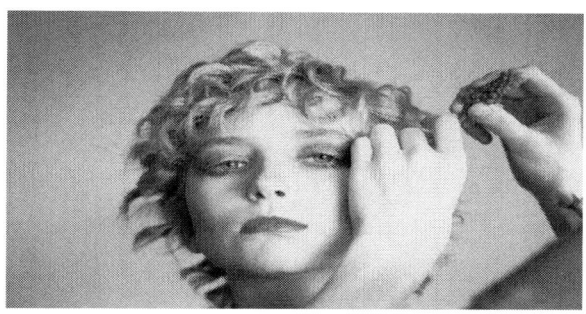

Gender Affirmation

If you are struggling with gender dysphoria, there are several avenues via which you can affirm your correct identity. Being able to express your true self is vitally important for your mental health, and while it can be daunting, there are both big and small ways to pursue gender transitioning.

The common perception of transitioning is that it is an all-or-nothing process—that someone is only transgender if they undergo full gender affirming surgery to change their physical sex features. But the truth is that transitioning can happen in degrees, and how far along this road you choose to go is entirely up to you.

Firstly, there is the option of social gender affirmation. This involves things like changing your name and choosing new preferred pronouns. You can also embark on legal affirmation by officially changing the gender markers on ID documents. Finally, medical and surgical affirmation is a possibility if you have access to adequate healthcare services and support.

Medical affirmation involves taking hormones or suppressants to halt the onset of puberty or to alter its consequences. For example, testosterone can help a transgender man build muscle, grow facial hair, and deepen their voice. Finally, there are several types of gender affirming surgeries that you can undergo: breast augmentation, facial feminization surgery, vaginoplasty, masculine chest reconstruction, and more.

You can—and should—try to seek advice and guidance on these different gender affirming tools. This is not to imply that you might be uncertain about your identity, although that is okay too. It is more to ensure that you are socially, psychologically, and emotionally prepared for these changes and ready to deal with any consequences. You can speak to your loved ones and friends, as well as a mental health or medical professional, about the avenues you wish to explore.

Who You Love

There is also a common misunderstanding that gender identity and sexual orientation are the same thing or that the two must be related. On the contrary, gender identity is about who you are and sexual orientation is who you love.

Born This Way

Sexual orientation is derived from the types of people you are attracted to, and both cis and transgender people can have a range of orientations. The attraction you feel can be romantic, sexual, or emotional, but it is driven by your brain structure and chemistry. What this means is that your sexual orientation is something you are born with. It is not something that you can control and change.

Most importantly, there is no right or wrong answer when it comes to attraction. Love is love, and embracing this part of yourself is a vital step on your journey of self-discovery and growth.

Of course, sorting out your feelings toward others can be confusing and challenging, and this is where experimentation comes in. Having different kinds of sexual and romantic experiences is normal for your age, and it is all part of the process.

It is possible to have a sexual experience that does not match up with your orientation, and you can be confident in your orientation without having had any sexual experiences. In other words, sexual orientation is not synonymous with sexual activity.

We will look more closely at sex in Chapter 9, but for now, remember that it is okay to go at your own pace. There is no rush to figure it out, and you should always put your physical and emotional safety first.

Sexuality Spectrum

Like gender identity, sexual orientation exists on a spectrum, and there is more nuance than most people are familiar with.

You will probably have heard of the two orientations at each end of this spectrum: heterosexuality (opposite sex attraction) and homosexuality (same sex attraction). But a person can also be bisexual, if they are attracted to both sexes, or asexual, which is when someone does not feel any type of sexual attraction.

It is also possible for your attraction to be less gender or sex specific. You could find yourself attracted to all genders and sexes or drawn more to a person based on their character or personality. This is called pansexuality, and it simply means that gender and sex are not defining features of your attraction or love.

A lot of people like to refer to their sexuality as fluid rather than choosing a certain label for themselves. This allows more flexibility for figuring out your likes and dislikes, and it is particularly helpful if you don't like the idea of trying to narrow yourself down to a box or category. All that really matters is that you are happy with your own orientation and can understand, accept, and express yourself as you are.

Being Queer

Where gender identity and sexual orientation do overlap is in the LGBTQIA+ community. People falling under the umbrellas of gender diversity and sexual fluidity have progressively united as one movement—often referred to as the queer community.

Being queer essentially just means that you are not cisgender or straight. For example, you could be transgender, nonbinary, bisexual, or asexual. You believe in and experience the fluidity of gender and sexual orientation, so you likely face the same challenges as others in this community.

The LGBTQIA+ community has long been the target of discrimination, prejudice, and harassment. Its members are regularly subjected to bullying and hate crimes. They can be denied access to key support services and basic healthcare. The suicide rates are higher from this group of people than the rest of the population.

Throughout history, mainstream society has struggled with deviations from what is considered normal, and many people fear what they do not understand. Fear and ignorance are the foundations of hate, but as the queer community grows in numbers and strength, it chips away at the mountain of transphobia and homophobia. Your generation is the best yet at accepting people as they are, which gives everyone hope for the future.

Coming Out

If you identify as queer, the LGBTQIA+ community can be your safe haven of support and guidance. It can provide resources for you to learn more about yourself, and you can form relationships with people who have lived through similar experiences. You don't have to *come out* publicly to be a part of this community, but seeing how others are able to live as their authentic selves may inspire you.

Coming out is the act or process of making others aware of your true identity or orientation. It is about self-disclosing so that you don't have to hide who you really are from your loved ones. Secrets eat away at the soul, and you deserve to express all aspects of your identity to the fullest.

Crucially, you do not have to come out until you are ready. You can take your time to adjust to yourself first. Start by making sure you are confident in yourself, and when you feel like it is time, you can share with those you are closest to. You can tell a friend who you know will support you. Or, consider telling a parent, sibling, or family member that loves you unconditionally. Try to be as honest and open as possible, and as hard as it sounds, be prepared for less-than-ideal reactions—shock, denial, and even rejection.

Not being accepted or understood by those you love is one of the hardest things in the world. All you can do is to give people time to come to terms with what you have revealed. Be comforted by the fact that those who truly love you will be able to set aside any differences and support you.

If it is the case that they never come around, remember that you have an entire community of people, spread across the globe, that you can turn to. Above all else, you have yourself. Self-acceptance and self-love are the most solid foundation you can create, and no one can shake your self-worth if you are happy and content in who you are.

CHAPTER 7

Self-Esteem

The previous few chapters were all about understanding your identity and figuring out who you are. But there is a key difference between *knowing* yourself and *liking* yourself, and we must now address this latter concept.

Low self-esteem is at the heart of many of the mental health challenges that teenagers face. Learning to accept and value yourself as you are is the foundation of good mental health, and moreover, it is a crucial life skill.

This chapter explores the idea of self-esteem, and begins by investigating its definition and potential causes. It then examines how low self-esteem can feel and the dangerous ways that it can manifest in your life. Finally, this chapter looks at the importance of building yourself up and establishing a good opinion of yourself.

The Foundation

Self-esteem is often thought of as the foundation of mental health. It drives your experience of and response to emotional challenges, and it underpins many of the mental health struggles that you may face.

As you learn more about yourself, you might have trouble accepting the ways in which you are different or want to be better. You can start to think that you are not good enough or that you don't measure up in comparison to your peers. It can be difficult to come to terms with the various parts of your identity, especially those that you cannot change or control.

Self-esteem is the culmination of all of these thoughts and feelings. It is a reflection of your self-worth, and it is all about how you view and value yourself. Essentially, self-esteem is your opinion of who you are, and it is how you feel about yourself when all external factors are stripped away.

Crucially, the thoughts and feelings that you have about yourself will affect your behavior. Self-esteem drives your beliefs about others and the world, and it determines how you act and respond. How you deal with new experiences, how you cope with pressure, and how you move on from mistakes—all of this is determined by your baseline opinion of yourself.

So, where does this opinion come from?

Your Origin Story

We are not born with an opinion about ourselves, so we learn how to think about who we are based on how others treat us.

Because we start off with no context, we have to take notes from others. As young children, we internalize how other people react to us, and we interpret the different types of feedback and signals that are directed at us. We watch how others operate, and we try to imitate them. We gather and absorb all the available information, and use it to form an opinion of ourselves and our role.

What this means is that your self-esteem as a teenager is still primarily derived from the external environment you experienced as a child. You haven't had a chance to create a more subjective opinion, and what you currently believe about yourself is mostly the result of what you have been told—explicitly or implicitly.

Criticism and Praise

The type of feedback and reinforcement you receive as a child plays a critical role in shaping your self-esteem.

For example, if you are constantly criticized or silenced growing up, you can begin to believe that your opinion is wrong or worthless. If you are punished harshly for your behavior or mistakes, you may develop a negative opinion of yourself. If everyone around you seems to think that you are a bad or naughty child, you think it must be true. Similarly, being regularly ignored or overlooked can lead you to think that you are not deserving of love and attention. Moreover, any kind of childhood abuse, neglect, or trauma can make you believe that you are not valuable as a person.

Praise, or the lack thereof, is just as important as criticism during childhood. A child that is praised or rewarded without real cause can develop an overinflated and ungrounded sense of themselves. A lack of consistency when it comes to positivity can create an unstable sense of self in a child, and the complete absence of praise can be extremely detrimental to self-esteem. If a child is never acknowledged for what they do well, they will begin to feel like their actions do not matter.

Of course, none of this is a given. Self-esteem is a tricky thing, and it is also very dependent on the nature of the child. Some children are naturally more sensitive to external factors. while others are able to turn adverse experiences into resilience more easily.

Parenting Styles

Even what could be perceived as an easy upbringing can cause low self-esteem, and good examples of this are the helicopter and snowplow parenting styles.

An overprotective parent who is very involved in your life likely loves you unconditionally and only wants to keep you safe. But this helicoptering and hovering can give you the impression that you are not capable of dealing with problems on your own. As a result, you grow up with a lack of confidence, and can believe yourself to be useless.

Similarly, a snowplow parent who tries to remove all your obstacles leaves you with no way of proving yourself. You might be told that you are strong and special, but you have no proof. Even with the best of intentions, parents can underestimate the value of facing and overcoming adversity. A child needs to learn that they are capable of independence, and the best way to instill this confidence is through experience.

Thinking Disorder

Whatever its cause, low self-esteem is considered a thinking disorder, and it is very common among teenagers. You are only just emerging from your childhood environment, and you haven't had much time to update your opinion about yourself based on other factors.

Low self-esteem can also be compounded by the uncertainty and confusion of adolescence. Your brain is still developing, you are still learning, and you are facing new and unique challenges every day. There is all kinds of praise, criticism, feedback, and reinforcement to internalize, and you can struggle to stay positive about who you are.

Having poor self-esteem is a really difficult way to live. It can be unbearable to dislike or hate yourself because you cannot escape from these feelings. Low self-esteem can make you feel worthless and unlovable. It leads you to believe that nothing you do is ever good enough and that everything about you is a mistake. You feel inadequate, weak, and small. You may start to degrade yourself and obsess over your flaws. It can be impossible to acknowledge any positive qualities you may possess, and you constantly look to others as better examples of how to be and act.

In addition to feeling and thinking badly about yourself, low self-esteem can affect your behavior in a variety of ways.

High Expectations

Perfectionism is one way in which low self-esteem can manifest. Driven by the belief that you are not good enough, you set continually higher expectations for yourself. You push yourself to succeed and achieve as a way of proving that you matter.

The trouble is that you can never truly satisfy yourself in this way, and you get stuck in a terrible cycle. You demand excellence, but even when you attain it, you are not fulfilled. No amount of success can make you proud of yourself because it doesn't change that core belief. Moreover, anything less than perfect requires punishment, and you are constantly riddled with guilt over small mistakes.

Self-Fulfilling Prophecy

You can also feel so badly about yourself that you do not even try. You are so entrenched in the belief that you can't do anything right that you become a self-fulfilling prophecy.

You refuse to participate because you think that you will fail. This fear of failure forces you to close yourself off to new experiences and opportunities for growth. You don't see anything good about yourself, and you are convinced that there is no point in trying. It feels like you need to quit anything and everything before you have a chance to disappoint yourself and others.

Feeling Incapable

Poor self-esteem detrimentally affects your sense of capability and competence. Your opinion of yourself drives how you function in the world and determines how much you believe in yourself.

If you are not confident in your ability to make decisions and cope with problems, you will not be able to operate with independence and agency. You are vulnerable to peer pressure and bad influences, and you can be riddled with insecurity.

Anxiety and depression go hand in hand with low self-esteem because you feel like you can't do anything right. Entering the world is terrifying when you have no faith in your ability to function on your own. You can struggle to make even the smallest of decisions, and this ongoing self-doubt can be exhausting.

Mistreatment

Low self-esteem can lead you to accept mistreatment and abuse from others. If you do not treat yourself well, you will not expect others to do so. It becomes easy to receive bad treatment from those around you when you think you deserve it. You can have difficulty forming healthy relationships if you don't have strong boundaries in place.

Allowing others to treat you however they please because you are just grateful for the attention is a recipe for toxicity. You have to love yourself first before you ask someone else to do it for you, and there is no way to outsource the job of feeling good about yourself.

Moreover, being unable to see value in yourself can warp your ability to value others. Treating others poorly becomes an easy outlet for your own self-hatred, and in this way, low self-esteem seeps into your relationships and interactions. If you cannot advocate for yourself, you will struggle to support others.

The Only Way Forward

At the very worst, low self-esteem can cause you to turn on yourself in harmful and destructive ways. Actively hating yourself can be incredibly dangerous, and you also need to be aware of how your subconscious dislike for yourself may be driving your behavior. We will look at self-harm in more detail in Chapter 10, but for now, it is crucial that you learn a few foundational truths.

You deserve to feel good about yourself because everyone deserves this. We all make mistakes, and no one is perfect. There is nothing wrong with you, and you are not a bad person. As long as you are trying your best to do good in this world, you are *good enough*. You don't have to prove your worth to yourself or anyone else. You are valuable by virtue of being alive, and even if you can't see it yet, you bring love, positivity, and beauty to those around you.

Furthermore, you are all that you have. You have to be enough for yourself because you have to live with yourself all your life. Accepting and loving yourself cannot be optionable—it must be inevitable. There is no other way, and the benefits of good self-esteem far outweigh the pain and exhaustion of self-hate.

Resilience

Good self-esteem is at the core of emotional and psychological resilience. If you can value and love yourself for who you are, you will be able to face life's ups and downs with courage, strength, and flexibility. Good self-esteem means you can endure disappointment and failure without falling to pieces. Your worth comes from within, and your identity is stable. External factors have less power over your mental health, and your core opinion of yourself remains consistent

Building this resilience is a process that takes time and effort. You need to unwind what you learned about yourself as a child, and must start anew with a fresh perspective. What matters is not what others think of you but what you think of yourself.

Building Self-Esteem

The best place to start when cultivating good self-esteem is to find and focus on your positive qualities. Think about your strengths and values, and decide what you really like about yourself. Embrace these characteristics, and make them the centerpiece of the opinion you hold of yourself.

Next, you need to start trusting and believing in yourself. Work on building your confidence and independence by making your own decisions and taking responsibility for your actions. Give yourself a chance to showcase how capable you really are, and let go of the belief that you aren't good enough.

Finally, you can use this new attitude and perception to set different boundaries for yourself and your behavior. Allow yourself to have reasonable standards when it comes to external achievement, and raise the bar in terms of the treatment you are willing to accept from others. Believe that you are innately capable and worthy of kindness and love.

Share Your Insights on *Teen Mental Health* — Your Review Matters!

Dear readers,

Greetings! We hope this message finds you in good spirits. We are reaching out to you because we know how valuable your thoughts can be, especially when it comes to a topic as significant as teen mental health.

In the heartwarming and insightful book, *Teen Mental Health* by Emily Grace, readers are guided through the challenging journey of caring for their moods and emotions as teens. The author's compassionate approach, paired with practical advice, creates a supportive resource for those facing the complexities of teen mental health.

We understand that navigating your emotions and mood as teens can make you feel alone at times. That's why your unique perspective, gaining from this book, can be a beacon of hope for others who are just starting their journey.

Your review can not only provide valuable guidance to fellow readers, but also support the author, Emily Grace, in continuing to create meaningful resources for those facing the challenges of dealing with their teen mental health.

All you need to do is scan the QR code and on the review page, write a few words of encouragement to the other readers and for the author. Your words mean very much to us. Thank you.

CHAPTER 8

Body, Eating, Exercise

Another significant factor that can impact both your self-esteem and mental health during adolescence is body image. Having a distorted body image can lead to a range of issues and challenges, so it is important to learn how to create a healthy relationship with your body from a young age.

This chapter begins by exploring the concept of body image—which factors influence a teenager's perception of their body and how a distorted image can impact mental health. It then looks more closely at different eating disorders, their features, and the thoughts, feelings, and motivations behind these behaviors. Finally, this chapter concludes with some hard truths that will hopefully inspire you to get help if you are struggling.

Body Image

Body image is the mental picture you have of yourself in your head. It is your perception of your body and its various features.

Concerns over your physical appearance are normal during your teenage years and beyond. How you look—and how others perceive you—is important to you, and that is perfectly natural. Everyone is allowed to take pride in their appearance, outfit, makeup, bodies, and so on. The real challenge is about getting to a point of comfort and being able to embrace yourself as you are.

Influence(r)s

There are a range of factors that could be affecting how you feel about your body right now.

Firstly, you are likely still adapting to the physical consequences of puberty. This process causes a lot of change when it comes to your weight, height, and body shape. Reaching sexual maturity can mean the appearance of fat, cellulite, stretch marks, and muscles in all new places, and your perception needs time to catch up to your physical appearance.

In addition to these natural influences, there are also more artificial pressures on your body image, especially for your generation. You are overexposed to the fakeness and filtering of social media. You have grown up with things like fitness culture and "thinspo," and all of these forces converge to create an unrealistic and unattainable perception of what a body can or should look like.

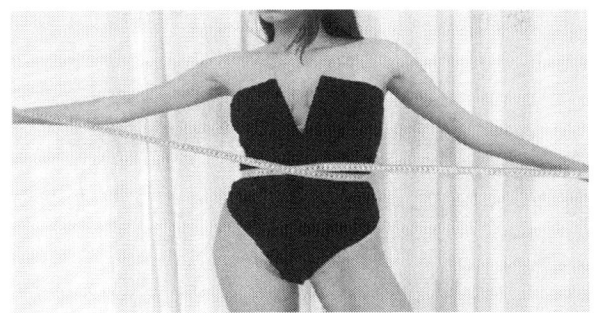

Young people today feel an unprecedented amount of pressure to live up to an ideal body type and to look a certain way. Achieving the right proportions is equated with happiness and success. You begin to think that if you can look like that influencer, then you can have the same lifestyle as them.

Distortion

The danger comes in when worries over body shape and physical appearance become obsessions. If you continually fixate on your perceived flaws and repeatedly compare yourself to an ideal, you will distort your own perception of your body. This can mean that you start to dislike your appearance or body shape to the extent that it causes you emotional, social, and physical distress.

Feeling uncomfortable and insecure in your body can lead you to withdraw from people or activities. You feel too ashamed and self-conscious to really be yourself, and you develop unhealthy ways of trying to cope. You can become obsessed with food, dieting, exercise, clothing, and cosmetics, and you might try to forcefully change the things about yourself that you don't like.

Dysmorphia

If these obsessions continue, the distortion of your body image can lead to a genuine cognitive and physical disconnect. You become literally incapable of seeing your body as it really is or as others see it. One possible consequence of this is that you develop body dysmorphia. This is a mental health condition characterized by obsessive thoughts about perceived flaws in appearance.

People who struggle with body dysmorphia see defects in parts and features of their physical appearance that others do not notice. Their brain exaggerates imperfections in their body, face, skin, hair, breast size, or muscle mass, and they become preoccupied with the idea that they are deformed or ugly in some way.

Body dysmorphia can cause a lot of shame, embarrassment, and anxiety. You become convinced that people will notice your flaws and laugh at you. You continually engage in things like body checking and excessive grooming, and you have considered cosmetic procedures and even surgery to fix what you think is wrong with yourself. You constantly compare yourself to others, and always need to seek external reassurance about your appearance.

To make matters worse, it seems like no one understands why you don't like this specific aspect of yourself. It feels like no one sees what you see—and, this is actually true. Your obsessions have distorted your body image, and your perception no longer reflects reality.

Eating Disorders

A similar process of distorted thoughts and feelings takes place when someone develops an eating disorder. At their core, eating disorders are mental illnesses, and they are driven by body distortion and dissatisfaction.

There are many different kinds of eating disorders, and the two that you are likely the most familiar with are anorexia and bulimia. Anorexia is self-imposed starvation through the restricted intake of food, and bulimia involves patterns of binging and purging food.

Another eating disorder commonly experienced by teens is binge eating disorder, which is characterized by episodes of deliberately overeating. Recently, there has also been greater acknowledgment of a condition called orthorexia, which is an obsession with healthy and clean eating.

Overlapping Features

Every eating disorder is unique, but there are several overlapping features and symptoms that could indicate a problematic relationship with food:

- obsessing over calories, nutritional facts, and food groups
- skipping meals
- lying and being secretive about food

- making excuses not to eat
- refusing to eat in front of or with other people
- feeling uncomfortable around food
- experiencing distress in grocery stores or restaurants
- abusing laxatives
- hiding or hoarding food
- weight changes and fluctuations
- losing your period
- strange physical changes like thinning hair, yellowing nails, and growing fur (lanugo)
- throwing up food
- exercising excessively

This last feature is characteristic of several eating disorders, and it is significant because it can also exist outside of your relationship with food. In general, exercise is good for your physical and mental health. But as with anything, moderation and intention are important.

Compulsive and obsessive exercise is a disordered behavior, so you need to carefully examine your motivations. Are you exercising because you enjoy it and it makes you feel good? Or, are you trying to punish yourself for something? Do you only exercise because you want to lose weight? Or, to counteract the calories you consume? Deep down, you will know the honest answer to these questions.

Compulsion

What you might be less sure of, however, is why exactly you are doing any of these things. Sure, you might not like your body or want it to be different. You may understand that these behaviors are compulsions that you can't control very well. You might even know that they are unhealthy and dangerous, but you keep doing them—*why?*

It can be difficult to uncover what is hiding underneath your eating disorder or to glimpse what is lurking behind your distorted body image. So, let's take a look at some possibilities.

It is possible that you have somehow managed to conflate your appearance with your self-worth. Like a perfectionist, you are trying to find an external way to value and evaluate yourself. You have come to associate thinness, weight loss, restriction, or whatever it might be with achievement, success, perfection, and being a good person. If you let go of these behaviors, you will be lost. You will need to face difficult questions about who you are and what makes you enough.

You could also be using your eating disorder as an expression of low self-esteem. You may need a way to punish yourself for other perceived failings and weaknesses. You can eat—or not eat—depending on whether you feel like you deserve it. In this way, you are constructing a system of checks and balances that allows you to keep score of all your rights and wrongs. You can even out the scale—in more ways than one.

Finally, it can be true that your eating disorder is simply a coping mechanism. You are using food and weight in place of emotional regulation, and your relationship with your body depends on whatever you are feeling at any given time. Your eating disorder is a mood stabilizer that helps you deal with the stress and mess in your head. It is the crutch you cling to as an attempt to control the chaos in your life.

You Are Not in Control

When you are living through the hell of obsession and anxiety that comes with suffering from an eating disorder, you *know* that something is wrong. It is more often parents and friends that need lists of warning signs and symptoms in order to really see what is happening—you are intimately familiar. The specifics might be baffling and the exact underlying reasons unknown, but deep down, you have a feeling that this path you're on is only going downhill.

The real problem with getting help for your eating disorder is that you do not want to change—not just yet. You might not believe that you need help, and you can think that you have everything under control. You'll just reach a certain goal, get to your target weight, and then stop.

You might also think that you aren't sick *enough* to get help. Maybe, you don't think that you're thin enough or that your behavior is all that bad. Things aren't that serious, and you don't want to make a big deal out of nothing. You may even believe that you don't deserve help and that you should be able to figure this all out on your own. Your self-esteem has sunk so low and you're so far down the spiral of an eating disorder that you believe you deserve this struggle.

Hard Truth

The hard truth is that eating disorders are incredibly damaging and dangerous, and no matter what you think, you are not in control.

The thought patterns and behaviors can be suffocating, enticing, tempting, and manipulative. But ultimately, there is no way to win with an eating disorder. No number on the scale will ever be low enough and no body shape is ever going to make you happy.

There is also no such thing as being sick enough because any kind of disordered or distressing feelings necessitate attention. In other words, you deserve a healthy relationship with your body, regardless of the intensity of your behaviors. Just as external thinness does not indicate health, a lack of visible symptoms does not mean that you aren't struggling internally.

Ultimately, you are going to have to let go of this coping strategy and find other—healthy—ways to make yourself feel safe. But you don't have to do this alone. Talk to someone about what you're going through, and ask for the help that you know you need.

In the end, we need food to live, and we live in our bodies. We are all that we have, so we must be enough for ourselves.

CHAPTER 9

Relationships, Sex, and Social Media

In addition to the thoughts and feelings happening inside your own head, you may have to face a range of interpersonal challenges during your teen years. Adolescence is filled with all kinds of new social situations to navigate, and certain relationships and dynamics can present unique difficulties.

This chapter begins by exploring how your relationship with your parents can change during adolescence. It then looks at friendship, and outlines the potential hurdles that teens have to clear when it comes to their peers. Next, this chapter highlights romantic relationships, and touches on topics like sex and toxicity. Finally, it examines the pros and cons of social media and concludes by encouraging discernment when interacting online.

Clashes

Why do teenagers fight with their parents so much? This is a common perception based on a lot of truth, and it is normal to experience conflict with your parents during these years.

As you get older, you might find that you do not want them to be overly involved in your life. You withdraw from them, and start to put emotional walls up. This distance can create further difficulties as your parents try to hang on even more tightly. You may also have the urge to rebel against their expectations and instructions and to deliberately make them angry. You still love them, of course, but their presence is suffocating, and you want your own space.

All of this is a natural consequence of your stage of development. You are trying to grow as a person, become independent, and create your own identity. But parents have the responsibility of imposing boundaries and limits in order to keep you safe. In this way, they often become the bad guy in your view—the only thing stopping you from living your life the way you want to.

You are also relatively egocentric at this age given your underdeveloped frontal cortex, so it can be hard to see that your parents are people too. They have their own emotions, perspectives, and challenges, and they are doing their best in raising you. Everyone has different approaches and parenting styles, and no one is perfect. They will make mistakes, just like you.

Honesty

If you are experiencing these difficulties with your parents, it is okay. You are not a bad person, and fighting with them doesn't mean that you don't have a good relationship. You can still love each other unconditionally, even if you don't always see things the same way.

The best way to approach any conflict is from a place of honesty and openness. If your parents are making decisions that confuse and frustrate you, talk to them about it. There is no harm in asking questions, and you can even challenge them on their choices as long as you try to remain respectful.

It is also important that you help your parents understand your point of view. Let them know why you are acting the way you are and why you need space and agency. Being honest with them will show that you are trustworthy and capable of independence. It will also establish a good foundation of communication for when you are in need of their guidance.

Safe Haven

Even if you don't feel like you need their support right now, having people in your life that you can lean on and trust is crucial. Everyone needs some level of comfort, guidance, understanding, and validation from others, and building a support network is the most effective way to achieve this.

During adolescence, it is often your parents who form the cornerstone of this safe haven. They love you unconditionally, and have your best interests at heart. As Chapter 11 will explain, your parents can be the ones you open up to about any mental health challenges you are experiencing.

It is also okay if you truly don't have a good relationship with your parents. If they are not in your life for whatever reason or your home life is complicated, this is not your fault. Moreover, it is not within your power—or your responsibility—to fix it. In this case, you can center your network of support on the other people in your life: peers, friends, family members, trusted teachers, coaches, or counselors.

Peers and Popularity

Speaking of peers and friends, these relationships can present a range of challenges in your teen years. Everyone wants to fit in, one way or another. You might want to be popular, or you may just want a group of close friends that you can hang out with. The need to belong is completely normal, especially during the fragility of adolescence, but it can create problems of its own.

For example, you might find it difficult to resist peer pressure during these years. You want people to like you, so you are willing to sacrifice your personal values. You may struggle to stand up for yourself and others, and it can seem easier to just go along with the crowd.

You can also find yourself in the midst of unmanageable drama when it comes to your friendships. Emotions are heightened, and everyone is picking and choosing who they like best. This instability can be distressing, and can lead to a variety of uncomfortable situations.

Bullying is another feature of teen relationships that you might encounter. If you struggle with shyness or introversion, it can be more difficult to make friends. People on the outside are often the target of ridicule and further ostracization. Loneliness and isolation can be extremely detrimental to your mental health. It can lead to anxiety and depression, and can compound any other challenges you might be facing.

It is also possible to feel alone even when you have friends, and this is because quality often outweighs quantity when it comes to interpersonal relationships. It can be better to have one really good friend rather than a whole circle of acquaintances.

Finding Your People

Making and keeping friends can be difficult, so here are a few tips.

Don't worry too much about what the majority think. Instead of trying to be a part of the popular group, focus on who you really want to be friends with. Pick people who have similar interests to you and who will share in your fun and enjoyment. Your friends should be people who make you laugh. They should build you up and make you feel good about yourself.

To find these people, you need to be a joiner. Unfortunately, friends won't just show up at your doorstep. Sometimes, you have to go out and find them. So, try to be open to new experiences and participate in hobbies and extracurricular activities that you enjoy. Not only will you find people who like the same things that you do, but you will also be able to cultivate a range of relationships with people from various walks of life.

Forming friendships is a great way to hone your interpersonal skills, so don't give up on your search. You will need relationships to practice things like honesty, forgiveness, compromise, and conflict resolution, and as mentioned, having a support network is crucial for your emotional and mental well-being.

Romance

It is not just friendships that can present challenging social situations for teenagers. This is also the time of your life when you first start to experience an interest in romance, love, and sex.

You are figuring out your sexual orientation, feeling the beginnings of attraction to other people, and may want to experience intimacy for the first time. You are curious about relationships and dating, but you may also be confused about love, sex, and what it all means. This is a normal part of your adolescent development, and it can be fun, confusing, distressing, exciting, and everything in between.

Virginity

One thing that tends to worry teenagers quite a lot is the concept of virginity. It seems like there is pressure from all sides. Some find it embarrassing to not have had any sexual experiences, while others are determined to abstain. The truth is that virginity is a social construct, and it really doesn't have to take up such a large place in your heart or mind. It can be as important to you as you want it to be.

Everyone has their own values when it comes to sex, and as long as you are being safe and responsible, there is no right or wrong answer. The *right time* really is different for everyone, and all you need to do is figure out what is right for you.

If you are in a close relationship and feel ready for sex with your partner, that's great. If you want to wait until you are older, committed, or married, that's perfect too. Sex can be with someone you love, like, or are simply attracted to. You can want to experiment with different types of intimacy, and that is normal and completely valid. If you are not ready for anything like that, that is okay as well.

Above all else, sex is a personal choice. This will be true throughout your life. You never have to do anything you do not want to. How far you go—and when—is entirely up to you.

Safe Sex

Ultimately, there are so many possibilities when it comes to sexual activity. There are different kinds of sex acts and various levels of intimacy. Sex can also mean different things to different people, depending on the situation or relationship. Sex can be about physical intimacy, an emotional connection, or both. It can be for fun, enjoyment, and pleasure, and it can take place outside of a committed relationship.

Most importantly, sex is not something to be afraid of. Fear goes hand in hand with ignorance, and you shouldn't be uninformed about sex, even if you are not interested in it. Being as knowledgeable as possible is important for ensuring you can fully consent and keep yourself safe.

Open and honest communication becomes important here, and you don't need to be hesitant or embarrassed when talking about sex. Speak to your partner, parents, peers, and friends, and ask questions to establish comfort and safety around the topic. The more you know and share, the more you will be able to determine your own readiness for intimacy. As you become familiar with the details and possibilities, it will be easier to tell what you are emotionally and physically ready for.

Of course, if you are preparing for any kind of intimacy, you should make sure you are informed about the essentials of safe and responsible sex: contraception, STIs, boundaries, and consent. You can educate yourself on all of these topics or get the information from a trusted source.

Avoiding Toxicity

Sex can be unsafe in more ways than one, and you should be aware of the possibilities surrounding abusive relationships.

The patterns you establish in adolescence will shape your future relationships, so you need to be wary of what is and is not healthy. Try to be conscious of how your partner—and even your friends—make you feel. A healthy relationship should make you feel loved and safe, not manipulated, put down, criticized, or unworthy.

It is a hard lesson to learn, but it is better to be alone than to be with someone who hurts you. If your relationship feels toxic, trust this instinct, and try to get out before you become stuck in a cycle of abuse. Remember that everyone your age is learning how to interact with others, but this is not an excuse for unhealthy behavior. You deserve to be loved in a way that makes you feel good.

Social Media

Finally, it is not possible to talk about teen relationships without touching on social media.

Social media underpins many interactions and relationships for your generation. It is often the primary vehicle through which you engage with your friends and partners, so it's important that we take a quick look at the impact of this lifestyle.

Pros and Cons

On the positive side, social media provides all new ways of communicating. You can stay in constant contact with your friends, and actively participate in their lives. Social media creates unprecedented opportunities to interact and share, and it can give you a sense of validation, support, and community. A lot about social media is also simply fun. You can express yourself in different ways, and can just enjoy the creativity of engagement.

The flip side of this coin involves some issues that we have already mentioned. It becomes natural to compare yourself to other people when you live online. The pressure to conform to expectations is amplified, and you are constantly confronted with a certain ideal about how to be, look, and act.

Social media prompts everyone to live performatively. It can be difficult to stay authentic, and it is easy to get distracted by likes, views, and friends. The danger is that you become over-reliant on external validation, which is a fragile and unstable way to build self-esteem.

Despite its possibilities for endless interconnectedness, social media is associated with increased isolation and depression. It can be easy to feel left out when you see what other people post about themselves and their lives. You can start to feel self-conscious about your lifestyle, and it can be hard to watch others connect when you feel like you don't have similar bonds.

Moreover, the anonymity of the internet provides new and cruel ways for people to hurt and abuse one another, and cyberbullying is an issue unique to your generation.

Discernment

With any kind of freedom, access, and independence, comes responsibility. You have your parents and friends to guide you, but you are also very capable of doing what is best for yourself—you just need to have the courage to stand out from the crowd.

If you find that certain levels or types of social media engagement are doing more harm than good, then log off. You can make the decision to cut back as a way of prioritizing your emotional and social well-being. It can be difficult to go against the grain in this way, but at the end of the day, your mental health has to be more important.

Remember, like anything, this can be a process of growth and learning. You don't have to quit all platforms and delete all your accounts. You can carry on engaging with the sites and activities that make you happy. You should simply try to be more discerning about the impact of social media on your life.

CHAPTER 10

Self-Harm

We have touched briefly on this topic in previous chapters, but now it is time to delve more deeply into the issue of self-harm.

If you are sensitive to this kind of discussion, you are welcome to skip ahead, but the goal here is not to be too specific or triggering. The focus will be on understanding the dangerous nature of self-harming behaviors and why it is so important to ask for help.

Teenagers self-harm for complex and diverse reasons, and this chapter will begin by exploring these behaviors and motivations in a general sense. It then emphasizes how self-harm can be damaging, addictive, and unsustainable. Finally, this chapter concludes with a discussion on the stigma surrounding self-harm. It is often the shame associated with these coping mechanisms that stops you from speaking out.

Driving Forces

Self-harm is the act of intentionally hurting yourself in any way in order to deal with feeling overwhelmed or distressed. The term usually refers to acts of physical harm, but it can also encompass behaviors that aim to inflict emotional or social pain.

In addition to causing physical damage to yourself, self-harm can include other risky behaviors: drug and alcohol abuse, getting into fights, unsafe or compulsive sexual activity, disordered eating, obsessive exercise, toxic relationships, and any other addictions like online gaming, gambling, shopping, or social media engagement.

Ultimately, there are all sorts of ways in which you can purposely hurt yourself. The really important question is *why*. Why do you feel compelled to engage in harmful behaviors? Why are you being driven to this extreme? Why does hurting yourself make you feel better?

Self-harm can be very unique in its causes and manifestations, but there is also some overlap in the driving forces behind these behaviors.

Self-Destruction

Self-harm can be about self-destruction. For whatever reason, you might have a compulsive need to self-sabotage that leads you to intentionally hurt yourself.

Depression, anxiety, and loneliness are all contributing factors, and self-harm is also closely tied to suicidal ideation.

Thoughts of suicide can make you feel hopeless, afraid, and filled with dread, and it is not hard to imagine that these emotions might drive you to dangerous behaviors. Moreover, not caring whether you live or die means that you don't place a lot of value on your life, body, and emotional experiences. Self-harm might not seem like a big deal when you are struggling with chronic apathy around life itself.

Punishment

Self-harm can also be about punishment. If you feel like you aren't good enough, this strong dislike for yourself can manifest in destructive behaviors.

As we have seen, low self-esteem drives many mental health challenges, and it can lead you to believe that you deserve to be hurt. Having expectations of perfection can mean that you need some way of penalizing yourself for failure, and self-harm is a tempting form of discipline.

Control

Self-harm might also be the only way you know how to cope with what's going on in your head. Maybe, you don't know how else to express the confusion and distress you are experiencing. Turning emotional pain into something physical can make it easier to deal with—it brings the inside to the outside, and makes your problem tangible and visible.

In this way, self-harm becomes your tool for emotional regulation. It is your response to any kind of discomfort or distress, and it is how you control your emotions.

Expression

You can also be looking to express something else with your self-harm. These behaviors could be about trying to get others to notice that you are hurting. You don't know how to say that you need help, and your self-harm is the only way to demonstrate how much you are struggling.

Your self-harm can even be a means of getting yourself to notice your own distress. It can be a method of feeling connected to your body, your life, and the world around you. Perhaps, your self-harm is the only way you can truly feel something, and you need it to bring yourself back to the present moment.

Finally, self-harm can be more about the aftermath than the act itself. Hurting yourself gives you a valid reason to look after yourself. In this way, self-harm becomes a means to self-care, and you don't know how else to justify taking care of yourself. You feel like you only deserve to be soothed if you can see that something is wrong.

Unsustainable

This whole book is about the different mental health challenges that teenagers face. The central message is that adolescence can be a really hard time. It is normal to experience ups and downs and to struggle with difficult emotions and situations. You might feel lonely, anxious, and depressed, and you may battle to find yourself and your place. A lot of this is a normal part of growing up. But feeling like you want to hurt yourself is not.

Self-harm is not a phase or a natural side effect of being a teenager. It is not something that everyone struggles with, and you shouldn't feel like it is the solution to any of your problems. The same is true for suicidal thoughts. You should never feel like your life isn't worth living, and if you are self-harming in any way, you deserve to get help.

Survival Strategy

The truth is that, whether you want to believe it or not, you are doing physical and emotional damage to yourself. There are long-term implications for your actions, and you are creating trauma for yourself that you will eventually have to deal with.

This is not to say that it is your fault or that you are to blame. More than anything, self-harm can be categorized as a coping mechanism. You have developed a way of managing complicated feelings and calming your mind. Self-harm relieves the pressure in your head, and provides an outlet for your self-hate. You find your heart and mind are calmer in the aftermath.

Self-harm is your survival strategy. You feel like you are doing the best you can to get through your pain. This may be true, but it is also an incredibly dangerous and damaging path.

Dangerous Addiction

Like any behavior that you depend on continually, self-harm becomes an addiction. By engaging with it any time you experience distress, you are creating patterns for your body and mind. Your psychology changes, and it learns to respond only to the pain and harm you are inflicting. Eventually, you will truly have no other way of making yourself feel better.

Moreover, as with all addictions, nothing will feel as good as the first time. You will always need more and more of the fix to get a response. The relief you find is temporary, and over time, your self-harm will no longer help. You will be able to see that the costs outweigh the benefits, but you will not be able to stop. In other words, there is no sustainable way to self-harm.

You can literally rewire the pleasure and pain centers in your brain if you follow the same patterns for long enough, and the cycle will seem never ending. The guilt and shame of engaging in the self-harming act only reinforces your distress, and you will feel continually compelled to continue on this path. In the end, what you think is helping you stay in control is really the thing controlling you.

Stigma and Shame

The first step to dealing with any addiction is to admit that you have a problem. You need to accept that your self-harm is not a sustainable or healthy way of dealing with your life. It is doing more harm than good, and eventually, it will not help at all.

The next step is to ask for the help that you need. When it comes to self-harm, this can be very difficult given the shame and stigma surrounding this topic. People struggle to understand self-harm, and you might even be at a point where you don't understand your behaviors either. You may also be too ashamed to talk about it anyway.

Self-harm is associated with shame, embarrassment, and guilt because it is such an intensely personal and private struggle. It is usually always a secret, so sufferers are not accustomed to being open about it. To make matters worse, self-harm can have visible and physical consequences that other people can see. You spend a lot of time hiding what's happening, which makes you feel constantly vulnerable and on edge.

Many young people who engage in self-harm keep it a secret because they don't want anyone to worry. You may feel guilty about your behaviors, but you also feel like you have it under control. You want to deal with things alone, and you don't want others to make a big deal out of it.

A Different Perspective

Shame is a difficult feeling to overcome, but you will have to find a way to put aside your embarrassment and guilt in order to prioritize your emotional and physical safety. It really is as simple as that. You are stuck in an unsustainable and dangerous cycle of addiction, and you have to get out.

One way to silence your shame is to think about your self-harm from a different perspective. For example, if you had a physical illness, you would likely find it easy to tell someone. You wouldn't be ashamed of breaking your leg or getting the flu. In much the same way, your self-harm is a condition that needs attention. It is a symptom of your emotional distress, and you deserve treatment for it.

You can also imagine how you would feel if you found out that your best friend was hurting themselves in the same way you are. Wouldn't you want them to get help? Wouldn't you urge them to tell someone? Of course, you would. You wouldn't want them to keep it a secret or to continue hurting themselves. You would want them to be happy and healthy, and you deserve to treat yourself with the same kind of love, empathy, and respect.

Finally, think about how you would feel about the self-harming behavior if someone else was doing it to you. Can you see how unhealthy it is? Can you see that it is a problematic way to treat anyone—including yourself?

Alternatives

The main point of these different perspectives is to understand that you have done nothing wrong. You are battling a mental health challenge, and self-harm is the manifestation. Even though you are doing these things to yourself, it is not your fault. You do not have to be ashamed, and you are worthy of help just like anyone else who is sick or struggling.

The final important message of this chapter is that help is out there. It is possible to stop self-harming and to find better ways of coping with life. There is medication that can control your impulses toward self-harm, and there are therapies that can undo your addictive patterns. You can also learn other strategies for managing your distress.

Ultimately, you do not have to keep hurting yourself. You deserve better, and better is out there.

CHAPTER 11

The First Step: Talk to Someone

The first step to coping with any kind of mental health struggle is to open up and talk about it. Instead of keeping everything bottled up inside, you should speak with someone you trust about what you are going through.

This chapter will guide you on how to do just that. It will explain why it is so important to open up about your problems, and it will explore your different options when it comes to choosing someone to talk to. Finally, this chapter looks at some of the specifics around sensitive conversations and how you can best prepare for this situation.

Speaking Up

By this point in the book, you have learned a lot about what people your age are going through. You now know that everyone struggles with something. There are numerous different challenges that you and your peers are facing, and the message should be clear—you are not alone.

This is also one of the most important reasons why you should speak out about your troubles. Someone else might be going through exactly the same thing, and you don't have to suffer alone or in silence. You don't have to be ashamed of your issues, and you don't have to be embarrassed about something that everyone deals with in one way or another.

Ultimately, even though talking about personal and difficult things can be scary and hard, the benefits will far outweigh any discomfort you might feel in the short term.

An Unbearable Weight

Speaking up is your first step to understanding what is really going on with you. You can lessen the fear, confusion, and stigma around your struggles by putting words to what you are feeling. Opening up is the best way to get all the complicated emotions and thoughts out of your head. You won't know how much of a relief it can be to let it all go until you actually do. It will be an unbearable weight off your shoulders.

Talking to someone else will also create opportunities for perspective, guidance, and support. This person can help you manage your emotions, and they can give you advice and clarity on how to cope with your problems. You can let go of all the secrets, stress, negative coping strategies, and start to get a real handle on things.

Finally, everyone needs someone to lean on. Mental health challenges can be isolating, and opening up is a chance to get the love and comfort that you need during this time. It is not your fault that you are struggling, and you are worthy and capable of feeling better.

Trusted Sources

Now that you've hopefully accepted that you should speak to someone about your struggles, you probably have a question—who?

Ideally, the person you choose to talk to should be an adult that you trust. You need to trust this person so that you can feel comfortable and safe when being honest with them. It is best that this person is an adult because they are more likely to have the wisdom and perspective necessary to help you. An adult has more experience and discernment, and they may have gone through something similar. They will have a better idea of what to do about your problems, or they will be able to find out.

Specifically, your parents should be your first choice. They love and support you unconditionally, and they want what's best for you. If it is possible for you to speak with one of your parents about your troubles, then start there.

Sometimes, this isn't an option, and that is not your fault. Your next best choice is to pick another adult in your life that you trust. This could be a family member like an aunt, uncle, grandparent, older sibling, or cousin. Or, you can talk to a teacher, coach, nurse, or counselor at your school. If you go to church, a youth group, or are part of a community organization of some kind, you can speak with the pastor or leader there.

Back Up Plans

As a third choice, you can also open up to your friends or partner, even though they are not adults. They might be experiencing similar struggles, and can relate to what you are going through. You can provide comfort and support for one another, but it is also important that you both explore other avenues for help. Your friends might have a different support network from you, and they could have an adult in their life that you can lean on too.

Finally, your last resort for help should be online. The internet is full of information and resources that can be helpful. But, like with your social media engagement, you need to be very discerning about what you see online. Stick to government and educational websites if you are looking for information. These will be trusted and reputable sources that focus on accuracy. They can also point you to other reliable resources, so make use of these recommendations when exploring support groups, crisis hotlines, and online chats or forums.

Friends and online sources can provide a lot of encouragement and connection when it comes to mental health challenges. It is good to feel like you aren't alone and that there are other people who understand what you are going through. Having these communities and resources is important, but remember that you should also be looking for a trusted adult to talk to. You still need someone in your life that you can speak with face-to-face, and someone who can be by your side as you work through your struggles.

How Are You?

We all get asked this question, often several times a day. When you are going through a hard time, these can be the words you dread the most because you never know what to say. "I'm fine" feels dishonest and inadequate, and you don't know how to say that you are, in fact, not fine at all. You feel like if you say something, your world will collapse—the floodgates will open, and there will be no going back.

But this is what you need. You need to open up to get it all out, and you have to start somewhere. This question is as good an opportunity as any.

It sets the scene, and you can take the chance to say how you really feel. A person's tone and body language when they ask this question will indicate whether or not they really want to know how you're doing. If they look or seem serious, they have probably noticed that you haven't been yourself. They are offering you a lifeline.

Crucially, you don't have to respond with exactly the right words. You don't have to summarize all the thoughts and feelings in your head in one succinct and profound reply. You can just say, "Not great actually," and take it from there.

This is just a starting point, and it can also be as far as you go in that moment. You don't have to dive right into the nitty gritty, and you can come back to the details later. The important thing is that you've taken the first step. Now, this person knows, and you have a foundation to build on later.

Sensitive Conversations

Of course, you don't have to wait to be asked. You can start the conversation yourself, and if this is the way you want to go, there are useful ways to prepare beforehand.

Preparation

Before jumping right in, give a bit of thought to what you are going to say. This will ensure that you don't feel overwhelmed in the moment and lose all your words. Start by thinking about your issues, and try to understand what it is that you want to communicate. You don't have to unravel all the details or come up with a solution. You just need to have an idea about your own needs.

It can be helpful to write down what you want to say or to practice saying it out loud. This will make you more comfortable with your thoughts and feelings, and when the time comes, it will be easier to get the actual words out of your mouth. Consider coming up with a specific conversation starter, and choose one thing that you want to express. This can be the most important thing—the issue that worries you the most—or it can be the least of your concerns—something small to get the ball rolling.

For example, "Mom, I'm really struggling with anxiety, and I want to talk about it with you." Or, "Dad, I think I might be depressed." Be direct and honest—rip off the bandaid.

It is also important to be clear about what you want from the conversation. Maybe, you just want them to know you are struggling. Or, you might want to talk more about the issue because you need guidance, advice, or reassurance. It is okay to bring something up, and then ask to come back to the topic later. You can say that you aren't ready for details or help. The important thing is that you make a start.

The final piece of preparation is to pick the right time and place for this conversation. You need your trusted person's undivided attention, and you want to choose a moment and setting that makes you feel safe. Everyone involved should feel as calm as possible.

If you feel like the other person might need time to prepare, you can always start by asking them to make time for you later. In this way, you have requested their attention and hinted that you need to speak about something important.

Expectation

If you are imagining how this conversation is going to play out, it is also vital to include a range of outcomes and responses.

Try to remember that you have been dealing with this problem for a long time. It may seem normal to you by now, but this is the first time your loved one is finding out. Or, maybe they're only now discovering the extent of the issue. Either way, keep this in mind, and give them a chance to adjust to the news.

Shock, confusion, and disbelief are common responses, and you should prepare yourself for all kinds of reactions. No one is perfect, and it is possible that someone is going to respond in a way that is less than ideal. If things are getting off topic and going downhill, you can remind your loved one of the purpose here—you need help, and you want to talk to them about what is going on with you. Do your best to be honest and open, and be prepared to answer questions.

Having said that, you can still decide how much you want to share at this time. It is okay to set boundaries if you are not ready to open up completely—just be sure to communicate this effectively. You can say something like, "I'm not ready to talk about that right now." Or, "Can we talk about it some more later?"

Ultimately, the first step will be the hardest. Once you've cleared this hurdle and everything is out in the open, you can start to get the help that you deserve.

CHAPTER 12

Getting Help

Speaking out about your mental health challenges can be a relief in itself, but it is also an important gateway to getting more help. Sometimes, talking about things isn't enough, and you need professional treatment. There are different options available depending on what you are struggling with, and it is best to seek the advice of a professional in order to determine the right path for you.

This chapter is all about treatment avenues for mental health. It begins with a discussion of the professional resources available and how you can go about seeking qualified advice. It then explores the types of therapy generally used to help people with mental health struggles, and it highlights the role of medication in this field. Finally, this chapter overviews intensive and alternative treatment options that may be necessary in certain situations.

Seeing Someone

Once you have opened up to the trusted adult in your life, they can assist you in seeking additional and professional support. Your parent, teacher, or coach will likely have more perspective, wisdom, and resources in this area, and they can be a good judge of whether or not you need to *see someone.*

If this phrase fills you with dread, don't worry. It is very normal to be reluctant about this, and even adults struggle to come to terms with the fact that they need help.

As we know, there is a lot of shame, embarrassment, and guilt attached to mental health problems, and it is natural that you might not want to talk to a stranger about what you're going through. You may also be struggling with overwhelming confusion about your experience, and you don't know how you would even begin to explain or express it all.

Exhaustion is another big deterrent when it comes to seeking professional help. You have been battling your thoughts and feelings for so long, and you've just about given up. The idea of having to go through everything again, starting at the beginning to try to figure out what's going on, makes you tired beyond words.

These are all valid and understandable responses, but they do not change the reality of the situation. If you are struggling to the point of needing professional help, your problems are not going to go away on their own. Even though it is hard, you should consider taking this step because you will feel better for it.

A Little Faith

It can be impossible to believe that anything can help you. You may have lost all hope that you will ever feel better. You may be too tired, scared, and confused to even care. But, now is the time to have a little faith—in the world and in yourself.

There are people out there who have faced the same terrifying feelings and thoughts, and they have managed to overcome these challenges. It is possible to heal, cope, adjust, grow, and thrive because people do it every day. Ordinary men, women, teenagers, and children make themselves extraordinary with their resilience and perseverance.

Moreover, you have to believe that those who specialize in mental health will be able to guide and advise you in the right way. This is their job and passion, and even if you can't see it, they care about your well-being. They have the knowledge, experience, and expertise to make you feel safe and understood. They are not the enemy, rather they can shine a light on your ability to save yourself.

Most of all, you must believe that you are strong enough to get help. You have survived your struggles so far, and by making it through each day, you prove your bravery. You are capable of taking this next step and facing up to yourself and your challenges. You just need to have some faith in who you are and what you can do.

One Step at a Time

Above all else, open and honest communication is the best way to make sure you feel safe on this journey. If your trusted adult suggests that you see a professional, talk to them about how this makes you feel. Together, you can come up with a plan that takes your emotional and physical safety into account but also prioritizes your comfort.

There are levels and degrees when it comes to professional help, and you can take things one step at a time. You can try one avenue, and if it doesn't work for you, you can try something else. It can be a process of experimentation and learning, and you can move at your own pace. If you don't like a specific person, treatment, therapy, or medication, you can try something new.

You just have to do your best to communicate how you are feeling and why. Remember that you have a say in what happens to you. Most importantly, don't give up.

Practical Steps

From a practical perspective, you might be wondering where to start with all of this. Where do you go? Who do you call? Who must you see? The medical and mental health profession is vast, complex, and often difficult to navigate. It can be hard to know what services you need, which are available to you, and how you can access them.

The easiest place to start is with a regular doctor. A primary care physician or general practitioner will be able to advise you on your mental health care options. You can make an appointment with the doctor you usually see, or you can visit someone new in your area. You can look up local doctors online or ask your friends or family if they know of anyone you can see.

Remember that you are not alone in all of this, and you can ask your trusted adult to make the appointment for you. They can even come in with you if you want or need the support. Going in alone is also an option if that would make it easier to talk, but the doctor will probably want to get the perspective of your parents if you bring them with.

The First Appointment

Just like you did in the previous chapter, start by stating what the problem is as clearly as possible. The doctor will ask something like, "How can I help you today?" You can reply with a prepared conversation starter: "I'm really struggling with my eating habits, and I think I need some help."

The doctor will then question you in a bit more detail about your symptoms, feelings, and thoughts. Even if it is uncomfortable, try to be as honest as possible. Remember that there is no need to be embarrassed, and they can help you more effectively if you give them all the information. The doctor might also conduct physical tests to rule out other illnesses and conditions, and they may administer a formal psychological or mental health assessment.

At the end of it all, the doctor will give you a recommendation of some kind. They might tell you what they believe to be the problem or diagnosis and how they think you should be treated. They may also refer you to a mental health professional like a psychologist or psychiatrist. A psychologist (therapist or counselor) is someone who is trained in and can conduct different kinds of therapy with you. A psychiatrist is a medical doctor who is able to prescribe medication.

Mental health treatment depends on the type of condition and the severity of its symptoms. Everyone is unique, and it is possible that your treatment plan will involve therapy, medication, or a combination of both. So, let's take a look at these—and other—treatment avenues in more detail.

Therapy

As mentioned, if you are referred for therapy, this will likely be conducted by a trained psychologist or therapist. This is someone who has studied theories of psychology and is qualified to offer you advice and guidance on how to manage your emotions, thought patterns, and behaviors.

A psychologist will usually open a session by explaining the rules of confidentiality. Usually, everything that is said between a therapist and their client is confidential and stays just between them. The major exception is if a psychologist believes you to be a danger to yourself or others. They can then breach the code of silence in order to get you more help or protection.

As a minor, the rules of confidentiality may be different depending on where you live and who your therapist is. It may be the case that they are allowed to discuss your sessions with your parents or legal guardians. They may even be obligated to do so depending on the circumstances. If it is not clear to you and the details of your privacy and disclosure are important, then you can simply ask the psychologist to explain.

Remember that you are the focus of this care and treatment, and your emotional well-being is the priority. You have rights—and responsibilities—even as a minor, so make sure the dynamic with your psychologist is clear.

Beginnings

Your first session will have to include another explanation by you as to what you think your problem is. The difference here is that a psychologist will be more interested in talking about your goals and outcomes for therapy than focusing solely on your symptoms. They will ask you what you want to achieve and how you want to feel, and you don't have to have all the answers right away. The goal of therapy is to work together to figure it all out.

The psychologist should also explain early on in your relationship what kind of therapy they conduct. There are many different techniques and variants, and some are more appropriate for certain conditions and challenges than others. If you are curious, you can ask about the options. You can even be referred to someone who specializes in the type of therapy that is best suited to you.

Above all else, you should know that therapy is a process. It is not a quick fix, and it will take work. You need to be patient, but it will all be worth it in the end—don't give up.

All of the Acronyms

Most psychologists conduct a form of psychotherapy, which is also known as talk therapy. The aim of this branch of treatment is to help you understand yourself and your problems. From this foundation, you can build new ways of thinking and coping.

A common variant of psychotherapy is cognitive behavioral therapy (CBT). This approach is based on the belief that how we think affects how we feel, which then impacts how we act. The helpful reverse of this is that we can change our behaviors and even our feelings by adjusting our thought patterns. To this end, CBT teaches you how to identify distorted ways of thinking so that you can regulate your emotions and create healthy behaviors.

Acceptance and commitment therapy (ACT) is another branch of talk therapy, and it is all about learning to accept what you cannot change. Acknowledging your emotions as they are enables you to find peace and contentment in your identity. ACT helps you to achieve mindfulness and match your behavior to your core values.

If you struggle with overwhelming emotions and instability in various areas of your life, then dialectical behavior therapy (DBT) might be your best option. DBT focuses on teaching you practical skills and techniques for tolerating distress, regulating emotions, staying present in the moment, and relating effectively to others.

You can also hone in on communication and relationship problems with interpersonal psychotherapy (IPT). IPT acknowledges the importance of others in shaping our mental health, and it addresses your struggles as symptoms of some kind of interpersonal distress.

Additional Avenues

Ultimately, therapy for mental health conditions is diverse and multifaceted, and there are options in addition to psychotherapy.

For example, creative therapy—involving music, art, and dance—is growing in popularity and success. Moreover, the next chapter will dive into detail about various self-care tools and lifestyle changes that you can implement in order to better manage your mental health independently.

Of course, medication and intensive or immediate treatment are also potential avenues that you can explore.

Medication

Mental health medication is a very personal choice, and it is important to get the advice of a psychiatrist if this service is accessible to you.

There are some cases in which medication may be the best option. Mental health conditions that are driven by chemical imbalances in the brain can often be effectively treated with a prescription. This includes antidepressant medications like selective serotonin reuptake inhibitors (SSRIs) and serotonin and norepinephrine reuptake inhibitors (SNRIs).

There is also a range of antianxiety medications and mood stabilizers that can help to control and relieve certain symptoms of emotional distress. Moreover, some neurodevelopmental conditions are best managed with medication. For example, ADHD symptoms can be treated with stimulant medications such as Adderall and Ritalin. Finally, certain chronic mental illnesses—like schizophrenia and bipolar I disorder—are generally treated with antipsychotic medications.

Caveats

It is crucial to keep in mind that, like with therapy, medication is not a quick fix or a cure. Unfortunately, you can't just take a pill and be happy. You will probably still need to delve into the details of your thoughts and emotions in order to achieve good mental health—which is why therapy is often used in conjunction with a prescription.

Sometimes, medication can be a one-off incident that gets you to a good enough place to start actively dealing with your challenges. It does not have to be a lifelong commitment, and you can try different combinations to see what works best for you. There is no one-size-fits-all solution, and there can be side effects associated with different types of medications.

Ultimately, medicating for mental health can involve a lot of experimentation, monitoring, and adjustment. But it can also really help you, so take the time to consider the options. Weigh the pros and cons, and maintain open and honest communication with your psychiatrist.

Intensive Treatment

Finally, it should be mentioned that there are more intensive forms of psychological and psychiatric care if you are experiencing a crisis.

Your doctor will notice if this is necessary, and they may recommend that you undergo inpatient treatment. This involves staying in a hospital or mental health institution where you can receive full-time care. Inpatient options are generally only recommended if you cannot take care of yourself or if you pose an immediate danger to yourself or others. For example, if you are struggling with a life-threatening crisis that requires urgent attention like self-harm, suicidal thoughts, and psychosis.

There are also specialized institutions that treat specific mental health challenges, such as eating disorder clinics and rehabilitation centers for drug and alcohol addiction. Treatment for these conditions can also take place on an outpatient basis. You can attend day programs or group therapy meetings in a hospital or clinic without having to live in.

You, or your trusted adult, can research specialized and specific treatment options, but once again, your doctor should be able to advise you about the services available. They can also refer you to community support, and you may be assigned a social worker or crisis management team. This will depend on where you live and what condition and symptoms you are struggling with. The important thing to remember is that the options are out there, and you deserve to get the help that you need.

CHAPTER 13

Helping Yourself

In addition to talking about your struggles and seeking professional treatment, there are many ways in which you can improve your own mental health. It's important to remember that, even though you might feel overwhelmed and exhausted, you have a lot of power to help yourself.

This chapter emphasizes agency, independence, and self-motivated healing and growth. It explores different lifestyle changes that you can implement in order to boost your physical and emotional well-being. It then explains a few practical tools that you can use to regulate your emotions, tolerate distress, and control your impulses. Finally, this chapter looks at several avenues for personal growth, including creative expression, mindfulness, and positivity.

Taking Responsibility

As we have seen, mental health is about more than not having a mental illness. It is a measure of your overall well-being, and it is influenced by a variety of factors. Good mental health means emotional resilience and distress tolerance. It is the ability to grow and the strength to accept and love yourself as you are.

Support from others in dealing with mental health challenges is vitally important. This book recommends that the first step you should take when feeling overwhelmed is to talk to someone else about it. But in addition to opening up, there is so much you can do to help yourself feel better.

The Importance of Agency

Being proactive about your own mental health is important for strengthening your sense of agency and capability. It is crucial to have confidence in your problem-solving abilities, and regaining a healthy level of control over your body and mind will improve how you see yourself.

Moreover, you need to play an active role in the state of your mental health in order to better understand how you think and act. Managing yourself is a vital life skill that you will need throughout adulthood.

Self-motivated healing is also the path that is most likely to be successful. If you set your own goals and make your own decisions, you are more likely to follow through. Whereas, if someone else is driving your treatment, you can feel trapped, forced, and incapacitated. You are probably not going to give it your best effort if you don't feel like you have any control. So, instead, take responsibility for your care, and put yourself in charge of your mental health management.

Basic Wellness

The first steps to improving your mental health are all things that you have heard before. You have to eat, exercise, and sleep well in order to feel stable and strong. This advice is common because it is accurate and helpful, and if you are at the beginning of your wellness journey, you should start with these basics.

Movement

Exercise is hugely beneficial to both your mental and physical health. It helps to prevent chronic illnesses and cardiovascular disease, and it lowers your risk of conditions like obesity, diabetes, hypertension, and high cholesterol.

From an emotional perspective, physical activity causes your brain to release hormones called endorphins, which boost your mood. It combats stress, anxiety, and depression by encouraging the production of dopamine and serotonin. Finally, exercise improves your body image and self-esteem, and it helps you to feel good about yourself.

It is recommended that everyone engage in at least 30 minutes of physical activity every day, and this can take the form of any kind of movement. You can join a sports team or take up running, cycling, or swimming. You can also do yoga, take a dance class, go on a walk or hike, or potter around in the garden—whatever you enjoy most. Ultimately, the type of moment is less important than getting into the routine of daily activity.

Food

When it comes to food, everyone's likes, dislikes, patterns, and habits are unique. Cultivating a healthy relationship with food is a process of trial and error, and not everyone is going to eat in the same way.

From the perspective of physical health, most of us understand the basics, even if we aren't too keen on them. We know that we should try to eat fruit, vegetables, and lean proteins and that too much fast, fatty, and processed food is not good for our health.

But what you might not have noticed yet is that different foods will affect your mood in different ways. Sugary and processed foods make most people feel jittery, irritable, and low. On the other hand, protein and whole starches will help you to feel nourished, motivated, and energized.

This is, of course, not a given or set rule that applies universally. Everyone has to figure out their own body. Start by trying to be more mindful of how certain foods make you feel, then simply do what makes you feel good.

Sleep

People tend to underestimate the importance of good sleep. Every adult needs between eight and nine hours of sleep each night, and sleep deprivation can wreak havoc with your emotional stability and physical health.

As such, it is important to establish good sleep hygiene as soon as possible, which means creating a set routine around going to bed and waking up. A great tip for everyone in this day and age is to shut off all devices and avoid blue light screens at least an hour before bedtime.

People

Building on these basics of wellness is the importance of your social support network. We have discussed this in previous chapters, but as a reminder, try to nurture relationships that make you feel good about yourself.

It is vital for your mental health that you make time to socialize. Humans are social creatures, and we thrive on interaction and connection. Even if you are a shy introvert, you cannot live in isolation. We all need people to lean on and laugh with.

Self-Care

Something else to carve out time for is self-care. This term is thrown around a lot these days, and there is value in understanding exactly what it means.

Self-care is whatever you do to look after yourself. It is how you help yourself cope with difficult situations. Self-care is about self-soothing, and it involves any actions or activities that calm you down in times of distress. These will be unique to you, but a great example is making time for relaxation.

Prioritizing leisurely free time is a particularly useful tool of self-care for teenagers. You can become so involved in your tightly packed schedules of academics and extracurriculars that you forget to enjoy your life. So, try to take the time to rest, relax, and recharge. Get out into nature, and take in the fresh air. Allow yourself to have fun, and figure out what you actually enjoy doing.

Healthy Coping

Another crucial aspect of caring for your own mental health is being mindful of how you cope with stress and distress. It is important to reduce any tendencies toward self-destructive, harmful, risky behaviors, and to create healthy coping mechanisms instead.

To do this, you can engage in the basic acts of wellness described above or create new routines that help you to manage your thoughts, feelings, and behaviors more constructively.

There are also various techniques and strategies that can be learned through the different types of therapy mentioned in the previous chapter. Let's look at a few examples that can be of practical use.

Emotional Regulation

Emotional regulation is a technique that helps you to understand your emotions so that you can cope with them more easily. This strategy is all about getting used to discomfort.

Difficult thoughts, feelings, and situations are inevitable, and no one is ever completely happy all of the time. Emotional regulation is about learning to experience your emotions instead of running away from them. You don't have to be afraid of your own feelings. Everything passes, and you are strong enough to endure. Over time, you will build up tolerance to distressing emotions, and you will be better able to cope with life's natural ups and downs.

To build this resilience from a practical perspective, you first have to practice identifying and labeling your emotions. This means putting words to your feelings and coming up with a name to describe your experience. You can then work on exploring the origins of this emotion and its impact on your thoughts and behaviors. The final step of emotional regulation is to move through the uncomfortable—to manage this experience without resorting to harmful or avoidant behaviors.

Distress Tolerance

In addition to sitting with the discomfort, you can also implement a distress tolerance tool when experiencing overwhelming emotions.

For example, the temperature, intense exercise, paced breathing, and progressive muscle relaxation (TIPP) tool is a useful DBT strategy. The goal of TIPP is to help you cope with a moment of intense panic, and its techniques are designed to stop overwhelming anxiety in its tracks.

The "T" stands for temperature. The next time you are feeling overwhelmed, try splashing your face with cold water, holding ice blocks in your hands, or taking a cold shower. The extreme temperature will provide a shock to your system that will help you to reset your body's responses.

The "I" in TIPP suggests intense exercise as a way of stopping panic, so consider a quick run or do a few minutes of jumping jacks on the spot. The aim is to raise your heartbeat and get your blood flowing so that you can come down from this heightened state of stress more naturally.

TIPP's first "P" stands for paced breathing, and this is a technique to manage your breathing and body. As you control your breathing, the rest of your bodily systems—heart rate, blood pressure, adrenaline—will follow suit and quieten down. To practice paced breathing, simply breathe in through your nose for a count of five seconds, then breathe out through your mouth for seven. Repeat until calm.

Finally, the second "P" refers to a relaxation technique, and the idea is similar to paced breathing—as you progressively relax your muscles, the rest of your body will calm down. Start this exercise by deliberately tightening the muscles in your feet. Hold this tension for five seconds, and then relax for thirty seconds. Repeat this process with the muscles in your calves. Then, your thighs, and so on. Work up your body progressively until you reach your facial muscles.

Impulse Control

Another DBT tool that is very useful in practice is the strategy of stop, take a step back, observe, and proceed mindfully (STOP). The STOP technique is about helping you consider your options before jumping into harmful behaviors. It is focused on impulse control and good decision-making.

The first step of STOP is to physically stop. This means that the next time you are feeling overwhelmed and find yourself tending toward a risky action, stop moving. Stand still until the urges pass and you feel more in control.

Next, take a step back. This means removing yourself—literally or figuratively—from the stressful situation. Give yourself time and space to process what is happening and to regain perspective.

Then, observe. Take a look at the situation more objectively, and consider the possible outcomes and actions. Weigh the pros and cons of each potential response, and try to figure out what you want from this situation.

Finally, proceed mindfully. This means using the calm and control you obtained and the information you observed to make a rational decision. Pick a way forward based on the objective facts and not your emotional response.

Personal Growth

This final section is going to touch on a few different strategies for enhancing self-esteem and finding peace and contentment. Here, you need to remember two important things.

Firstly, good self-esteem is the foundation of good mental health. You need to be able to love and accept yourself as you are because you are all that you have.

Secondly, uncertainty and discomfort are facts of life. Good mental health is not about never feeling bad. It is about being able to work through the negativity and come out stronger on the other side.

Creativity

One way of learning to love yourself is to continually discover who you are through creative expression.

Journaling is a great tool for this self-discovery, but you can engage in any form of expression you like: music, art, photography, dance, community service, culture, nature, spirituality, and so on.

The goal is simply to explore everything about yourself—your likes, dislikes, strengths, weakness, impulses, drives, fears, thoughts, feelings, emotions, dreams, anxieties, and goals for the future. Use this as a way of discovering new and interesting things about your identity, and hold these qualities up to the light. Value yourself for who you are.

Acceptance

You should also try to practice letting go. Radical acceptance is a philosophy of accepting what you cannot change and allowing some things to just be as they are.

Life is full of change, nuance, and the unknown. You can feel compelled to exert control and uncover all the mysteries that make you uncomfortable. But at some point, you are going to have to let go.

You can't force yourself to be a different person. You can't make someone love you. You can't know what happens after you die. Some things are just out of your control. So, practice being at peace with this. Say to yourself, "It is what it is." Move on.

Mindfulness

Mindfulness is another philosophy of acceptance. It is about living in the present moment and relinquishing control over the past and future. You can conquer a lot of depression, anxiety, and fear by focusing solely on where you are now and what you are doing at this time.

Observe your day-to-day life in more detail. Describe what you see and do, and participate mindfully in each and every moment. Let go of the need to judge every thought and feeling and to analyze everything that happens to you. Forget about the *right way* to do something, and embrace what actually works. Fully experience the now.

Positivity

Finally, when managing your own mental health, never underestimate the value of positivity. Being able to think and act optimistically in the face of external obstacles is key to emotional resilience. You can take back your power by controlling your outlook.

Positive affirmations and mantras are a good way to implement this attitude in practice. Say to yourself each day, "I am strong and capable," "I am healthy and healing," and "I am doing my best."

Allow yourself to make mistakes. Let yourself be imperfect. Fail so that you can learn how to do things differently. Messing up is part of being human, and punishing yourself for your mistakes is not going to help you grow. Instead, try to embrace your learning curves with positivity.

Above all, balance, flexibility, and moderation are some of the most crucial skills to acquire. It will take effort and patience, but don't give up. And, don't be so hard on yourself—you are still growing. There is time, hope, and help available, and you are not alone.

CHAPTER 14

A Note to Parents

To the parents (teachers, counselors, coaches, caregivers, and guardians) who have been reading along with us, this chapter is for you. You are crucial pillars of support when it comes to your teenager's mental health. There are many different ways in which you can provide comfort and encouragement, and this chapter is all about your role in helping your child cope with their thoughts, feelings, and struggles.

It begins with a discussion of warning signs that can differentiate normal and abnormal adolescent behavior, and it provides guidance on how to know when to step in. This chapter then explores how to talk to your teen about mental health—what to say, how to respond, and what to do next. Finally, it looks at ideas for creating a more open and honest environment around mental health in general.

Warning Signs

As this book has explained, adolescence is filled with challenges and changes. It is a transitionary period of emotional and physical growth, and teens are faced with a number of questions about who they are, what they are feeling, and what they want.

It is normal for you to see inconsistency in your teen. Their moods fluctuate, and their identity is flexible and fluid. They may pick and choose hobbies, drop friends, lose interest, withdraw, and fight with you in a way that you have never seen before.

While it can be hard to deal with, a lot of this is normal. It is part of the process of growing up, and it is natural for your teen to pull away and seek independence—as difficult as this may be for you.

Degree of Change

But all of this change can make it challenging to know when there really is a problem. How can you spot a mood disorder in a moody teen? How do you know they are struggling with their gender identity or sexuality when they seem to put on a brand-new character every day? How can you protect them from self-harm and risky behavior if they're keeping it a secret?

The key is to focus on the degree of change in your child, as well as the extent of negative behaviors and emotions that come along with that change. For example, if they are *always* angry, irritable, or down and you never seem to see a happier side to them anymore, then they may have a problem. Similarly, if they struggle consistently with eating, sleeping, and fulfilling their responsibilities, this may be indicative of a deeper issue.

Other signs to look out for include withdrawal from friends and a lack of interest in socializing. Your teen may cancel plans and lose enthusiasm for their academic work, sports, or cultural activities. They could also become obsessive and controlling, riddled with anxiety about school or their social group.

You may even see explicit symptoms of a mental health struggle like alcohol and drug abuse, sexual activity, or self-harm. These behaviors are not vapid or selfish bids for attention—they are cries for help and a sign that something is wrong.

Ultimately, you know your child best, and you can rely on your parental intuition as well. If something feels off, then trust this instinct.

Taking Action

Once you've noticed that there could be a problem, it can also then be difficult to know when to intervene. You want to give your child independence and space to grow, but you also want to protect them from the world and themselves. Moreover, mental health can be scary, confusing, and uncomfortable, and it is understandable that you might be reluctant to pry.

But at the end of the day, nothing is too big or too small to talk about. Mental health shouldn't be taboo, and your hesitance may only be reinforcing the shame, stigma, and guilt that your child is experiencing. This is not to say that you are in any way responsible for your child's suffering. But they do learn and internalize a lot of behavior by watching you, so try to be mindful of your approach to mental health. It may be time for you to be brave on their behalf.

The best thing to do if you are worried about your teen is to get everything out in the open. Make sure you are informed, prepared, and open-minded, and be ready to provide reassurance and support. Then—with care, empathy, and some caution—you can broach the topic.

Starting a Conversation

It can be hard to know where to start with this as well—what do you say?

One way to get your teen to open up is to regularly ask them how they are doing. As we saw in Chapter 10, "How are you?" can be the perfect conversation starter. It gives them an opportunity to bring up whatever might be on their mind, and lets them know that you are there and willing to listen. Try not to be too persistent, invasive, or threatening in your questioning. Instead, simply focus on communicating the consistency and openness of your presence.

You can also start a conversation with your teen about their mental health by using observations you have made. For example, you may have noticed them pulling away from their friends or quitting their favorite activities. Ask them about what you see going on with them, and follow it up with, "Do you want to talk about it?"

Similarly, instead of noting something about their behavior or mood, you can also share how you might be feeling. Try telling them honestly that you are worried about them, and you want to know a bit more about what's going on in their life.

Your final option for approach is to be direct. This is an especially good idea if you suspect dangerous behavior or a problem that your teen might be very reluctant to bring up on their own. Try to be gentle and nonjudgmental while getting straight to the point: "Have you ever thought about hurting yourself?"

Reactions

How you respond in these situations is equally important, so let's go over a few things to remember.

It's crucial that you give your teen your full attention during these conversations. Show them that you are actively listening by making eye contact and having open body language. Make sure that you acknowledge their emotions and experience, and tell them that you can see they are feeling overwhelmed or distressed.

It is also best that you try to manage your own emotions. It can be very difficult to see your child suffering or to hear about how they have been struggling. But it is important that you stay in control of your knee-jerk, immediate reactions—try to avoid anger, judgment, and dismissal.

Moreover, do your utmost not to make the situation about you. "Why didn't I notice?" or "Why didn't you tell me sooner?" These responses will only amplify your teen's guilt about their situation. Remember that this is no one's fault, and it is not a reflection of you as a parent. Most importantly, you and your child need to work together to cope, so reverting to a blame game is not helpful.

Above all else, your role here is to provide comfort and reassurance. Your child is likely scared and confused, and they need you to tell them that everything is going to be okay. So, tell them that. Let them know that you will help them get through this and that you will be with them every step of the way. Thank them for opening up, and acknowledge how hard that must have been. Give them hope that they will feel better soon.

Next Steps

As mentioned in chapters 10 and 11, you can play an important role in facilitating your child's mental health treatment. You are often the gatekeeper to professional help, and your teen will likely rely on you to make many of these decisions.

Of course, this is a big responsibility, but you do not have to go through it alone. Talk to your spouse, family, parents, and friends, and seek out the advice of your own doctor. It is also crucial that you try to include your teen in this process as a way of maintaining their agency and independence. Remember that this is all about their care and well-being, and having control over what happens to them will help them to feel better about themselves and their situation.

When deciding on next steps, try to keep as many options open as possible. Start with a primary care physician, and take all of their referrals into account. Consult a second opinion if need be, and be ready to go through the treatment process with your child. It will take time and effort from both of you, but they will need to know that you are in this together.

By the same token, be ready to face resistance from your teen. They may be reluctant to get professional help in the midst of all their shame, confusion, and exhaustion. Here, you can bring a healthy and helpful perspective by considering the long term. You don't want your child to carry these feelings, thoughts, and struggles with them into their adulthood. You don't want them to rely on dangerous and harmful coping mechanisms all their life.

So, even though it is tough in the short term, you know that getting help is for your teen's own good. It is better to address mental health problems as soon as possible, before they fester and mutate. The longer a secret is kept, the harder it will be to overcome.

Creating a Culture

In a more general sense, it will also be helpful to your child if you can create an accepting, validating, and open environment around mental health. Struggling doesn't have to happen in secret. Mental illness does not have to be scary, and questioning who you are and what you want is not shameful.

All in This Together

To transform mental health into an approachable topic, you can start by leading by example. This means talking more about your own challenges and experiences. Share your difficult thoughts and uncomfortable feelings, and try to normalize the idea of mental health struggles.

At their young age, teenagers don't have the context or experience to understand that what they are feeling is not new or unique. This is where you come in. Help your teen understand that they are not alone—everyone struggles with something.

Crucially, when sharing your own troubles, remember to stay age appropriate, and don't overwhelm or frighten your child. Don't overshare or try to emotionally rely on them. Moreover, be careful not to steal the spotlight too much. It is a fine line, but your role here is as a parent. You are not looking for your child to support you. You are modeling good behavior.

On that note, try to bring the focus to how you cope with your mental health challenges. Show your teen what you do to handle distress in a healthy way, and make mental health a collaborative effort. Encourage your family to check in on one another and to make time for each other. Share and brainstorm ideas for managing thoughts, emotions, and behaviors.

Validating Space

It is also so crucial to stay mindful of your parenting style. Fostering independence and agency is vitally important for teenagers, so try to avoid helicoptering and snowplowing. You love your teen unconditionally, and you want to protect them. But if you rob them of their chance to strive and thrive, you are hurting them in the long run.

You cannot face every battle for your child, and you have to learn to take a step back. The key is not to disappear entirely. The ideal parenting style is for you to act as a lighthouse—serve as an example, provide support through the darkness, and shine a light on the way out. In short, make sure your teen knows that you are always there if they need you.

Validation is an effective way to support your teen without hovering over or bulldozing their independence. Validation is about using words to remind your child that they are loved no matter what. It is about letting them know that you accept their identity and expression. You can validate your child by making time for them and giving them your full attention at crucial moments. You can acknowledge their experience by being present and listening to what they have to say. Validation is also about praising your child when they do well and prompting them to take responsibility for their choices.

Finally, a really important way to foster good mental health is to allow your teen to rest. Encourage self-care, and model this behavior by looking after yourself. Many of the same messages in this book apply to you as well. We are all human, imperfect, and capable of growth. We are allowed to make mistakes, change, and adapt. Ultimately, honesty and empathy are your best approaches when it comes to mental health—both your child's and your own.

Conclusion

By this point, you should have a much better understanding of yourself and your mind. The hope is that you have managed to uncover what your problem might be—what you are struggling with and why you feel or act the way you do.

Furthermore, you know now what you can do about it all. You have explored the options available, and the only thing left to do is to take that first step. Open up, and talk about what's going on in your head. Let someone help you and figure out how best to help yourself.

You are strong, capable, and resilient. You will get through the dark times, and can come out shining on the other side. Remember your worth, and hold on to the belief that you deserve to be happy.

Recap

If you are wanting to revisit certain sections or issues, here's a reminder of what we covered in this book.

Chapter 1 was a summary of the different challenges that teenagers face, including the biological, emotional, and social changes you experience during this time.

Chapter 2 was all about anxiety disorders—their symptoms and causes—as well as the roles of perfectionism, pressure, and perception. Next, we looked at mood swings and disorders, and Chapter 3 covered depression, mania, bipolar disorder, and burnout.

Chapter 4 focused on neurodiversity and ADHD, and Chapter 5 explored issues around personality and identity. The next chapter followed up with a discussion of gender identity, sexual orientation, and the LGBTQIA+ community.

Chapter 8 moved on to explore body image, eating disorders, and exercise. Chapter 9 looked at relationships, including friendships and romance, and touched on sex and social media. The final chapter of part one centered on self-harm and self-destructive behaviors.

Part two began by encouraging you to talk to a trusted adult about your problems, and Chapter 11 outlined how to start this kind of sensitive conversation. Chapter 12 was all about the professional help available for mental health problems, including therapy and medication.

Finally, we looked at self-care and self-motivated mental health management in Chapter 13. (Chapter 14 was for parents, but you can read that section if you want insight into what yours might be thinking or feeling).

Glossary

Body dysmorphia: Obsession over perceived flaws in appearance.

Body image: Your perception of your body and its characteristics.

Burnout: Physical and emotional exhaustion due to stress.

Cisgender: Someone whose sex and gender are the same.

Gender dysphoria: Psychological, emotional, and social distress experienced when your gender does not match your sex assignment.

Gender expression: Outward expression of gender.

Gender identity: Psychological and social experience of gender.

Generalized anxiety disorder: Constant anxiety with no specific trigger.

Identity: Confluence of factors making up who you are.

Mania: Feeling euphoric and unusually happy or irritable.

Mental health: Measure of psychological, social, emotional, and physical well-being.

Neurodiversity: Atypical cognitive development and processes.

Personality: Innate characteristics driving your thoughts and behavior.

Psychiatrist: Medical doctor specializing in mental health.

Psychologist: Someone trained in the field of psychology.

Psychotherapy: Type of therapy involving talking about your thoughts, feelings, and behaviors.

Puberty: Process of physical and sexual maturation experienced in early adolescence.

Self-care: Self-soothing activities.

Self-esteem: Your opinion of yourself.

Self-harm: Deliberately hurting yourself.

Sex: Biological designation at birth.

Sexual orientation: Who you love and are attracted to.

Social anxiety disorder: Anxiety triggered by social situations and interactions.

Stigma: Shame and guilt associated with something.

Transgender: Person whose sex and gender identity are not the same.

References

American Psychiatric Association. (n.d.). What are anxiety disorders? https://www.psychiatry.org/patients-families/anxiety-disorders/what-are-anxiety-disorders

American Psychiatric Association. (n.d.). What is gender dysphoria? https://www.psychiatry.org/patients-families/gender-dysphoria/what-is-gender-dysphoria

American Psychological Association. (2006, June 1). Just the facts about sexual orientation and youth. https://www.apa.org/pi/lgbt/resources/just-the-facts

American Psychology Association. (2019, October 24). How to help children and teens manage their stress. https://www.apa.org/topics/children/stress

Angel, T. (2021, October 13). Everything you need to know about ADHD. Healthline. https://www.healthline.com/health/adhd

Beresin, E. (2022, June 3). Low self-esteem in adolescents: what are the root causes? Psychology Today.

https://www.psychologytoday.com/za/blog/inside-out-outside-in/202206/low-self-esteem-in-adolescents-what-are-the-root-causes

Carloni, K. (2022, November 8). Personality disorders in teens: signs, symptoms, and treatment. Choosing Therapy. https://www.choosingtherapy.com/personality-disorders-teens/

Centers for Disease Control and Prevention. (2020, November 24). Mental health. https://www.cdc.gov/healthyyouth/mental-health/index.htm

Cherry, K. (2023, May 1). How personality impacts our daily lives. Verywellmind. https://www.verywellmind.com/what-is-personality-2795416

Child Mind Institute. (2023, January 17). Identifying mania in kids and teens. https://childmind.org/article/identifying-mania-in-kids-and-teens/

Chung, R. J. (2023, July 31). Teen mental health: how to know when your child needs help. Healthychildren.org. https://www.healthychildren.org/English/ages-stages/teen/Pages/Mental-Health-and-Teens-Watch-for-Danger-Signs.aspx

Cleveland Clinic. (2015, April 1). Nuerodivergent. https://my.clevelandclinic.org/health/symptoms/23154-neurodivergent

Cleveland Clinic. (2023, May 1). Adolescent development. https://my.clevelandclinic.org/health/articles/7060-adolescent-development

DBT Tools. (n.d.). STOP skill. https://dbt.tools/emotional_regulation/stop.php

Dialectical Behavior Therapy. (2018, December 30). T10: TIPP. https://dialecticalbehaviortherapy.com/distress-tolerance/tipp/

Ehmke, R. (2016, February 24). What is an eating disorder and when to worry. Child Mind Institute. https://childmind.org/article/when-to-worry-about-an-eating-disorder/

Explore Psychology. (2023, October 12). ABCD personality types: characteristics of the four types. https://www.explorepsychology.com/abcd-personality-types-characteristics-of-the-four-types/

Grohol, J. M. & Cox, J. (2022, March 31). What are the big 5 personality traits? PsychCentral. https://psychcentral.com/lib/the-big-five-personality-traits

Healthdirect. (2023, September 7). Anxiety in teenagers. https://www.healthdirect.gov.au/anxiety-in-teenagers

Kassel, G. (2023, April 20). Teenagers having sex isn't inherently bad or harmful—here's why. Healthline. https://www.healthline.com/health/is-teenage-sex-bad-for-them

Kort, J. (2020, October 2). Bisexuality, pansexuality, asexuality, and sexual fluidity. Psychology Today. https://www.psychologytoday.com/za/blog/understanding-the-erotic-code/202010/bisexuality-pansexuality-asexuality-and-sexual-fluidity

Mayo Clinic. (2022, February 26). Teens and social media use: what's the impact? https://www.mayoclinic.org/healthy-lifestyle/tween-and-teen-health/in-depth/teens-and-social-media-use/art-20474437

Mayo Clinic. (2022, August 12). Teen depression. https://www.mayoclinic.org/diseases-conditions/teen-depression/symptoms-causes/syc-20350985

Mayo Clinic. (2022, December 13). Body dysmorphic disorder. https://www.mayoclinic.org/diseases-conditions/body-dysmorphic-disorder/symptoms-causes/syc-20353938

Mental Health America. (n.d.). Medication. https://mhanational.org/medication

Miller, C. (2021, June 30). How anxiety affects teenagers. Child Mind Institute.

https://childmind.org/article/signs-of-anxiety-in-teenagers/

Mind. (n.d.). Coping with self-harm—for 11-18 year olds. https://www.mind.org.uk/for-young-people/feelings-and-experiences/coping-with-self-harm/

National Institute of Mental Health. (n.d.). Attention-deficit/hyperactivity disorder in children and teens: what you need to know. https://www.nimh.nih.gov/health/publications/attention-deficit-hyperactivity-disorder-in-children-and-teens-what-you-need-to-know

National Institute of Mental Health. (n.d.). Teen depression: more than just moodiness. https://www.nimh.nih.gov/health/publications/teen-depression

NHS. (2021, February 4). Worried about your teenager? https://www.nhs.uk/mental-health/children-and-young-adults/advice-for-parents/worried-about-your-teenager/

NIH MedlinePlus Magazine. (2023, May 16). Teens are talking about mental health. https://magazine.medlineplus.gov/article/teens-are-talking-about-mental-health

Psychology Today. (2009, March 17). Identity. https://www.psychologytoday.com/za/basics/identity

Psychology Today. (n.d.) Parenting teenagers. https://www.psychologytoday.com/intl/basics/parenting/parenting-teenagers

Raisingchildren.net.au. (2022, December 31). Mental health therapies and treatment plans for pre-teens and teenagers. https://raisingchildren.net.au/pre-teens/mental-health-physical-health/mental-health-therapies-services/mental-health-therapies-for-teens

Resnick, A. (2023, July 5). What does it mean to be neurodivergent. Verywellmind. https://www.verywellmind.com/what-is-neurodivergence-and-what-does-it-mean-to-be-neurodivergent-5196627

TeensHealth. (2022, November 2). I think I have a mental health problem. Who can I talk to? https://kidshealth.org/en/teens/mhealth-care.html

Unicef. (n.d.). Four things you can do to support your teen's mental health. https://www.unicef.org/parenting/health/four-things-you-can-do-support-your-teens-mental-health

Witmer, D. (2023, September 12). 9 signs of burnout in teenagers. Verywellmind. https://www.verywellmind.com/ten-signs-your-teenager-is-burning-out-2611230

World Health Organization. (2021, November 17). Mental health of adolescents.

https://www.who.int/news-room/fact-sheets/detail/adolescent-mental-health

Youngminds. (n.d.). A guide for young people: self-harm. https://www.youngminds.org.uk/young-person/my-feelings/self-harm/

Image References

Alexander Grey. (2019, April 22). Portrait of woman wearing teal eyelashes. [Image]. Pexels https://www.pexels.com/photo/portrait-of-woman-wearing-teal-eyelashes-2212718/

Andrea Piacquadio. (2020, February 22). Calm woman in lotus pose meditating after awakening at home. [Image]. Pexels. https://www.pexels.com/photo/calm-woman-in-lotus-pose-meditating-after-awakening-at-home-3791634/

Andrea Piacquadio. (2020, February 26). Woman in gray tank top. [Image]. Pexels. https://www.pexels.com/photo/woman-in-gray-tank-top-3812757/

Cottonbro studio. (2020, April 7). Woman in black hoodie sitting on brown wooden chair. [Image]. Pexels. https://www.pexels.com/photo/woman-in-black-hoodie-sitting-on-brown-wooden-chair-4100485/

Cottonbro studio. (2021, May 27). Photo of people engaged on their phones. [Image]. Pexels.

https://www.pexels.com/photo/photo-of-people-engaged-on-their-phones-8088684/

Fauxels. (2019, November 15). Man and woman holding hands. [Image]. Pexels. https://www.pexels.com/photo/man-and-woman-holding-hands-3228726/

FransA. (2019, June 4). Pride month gathering. [Image]. Pexels. https://www.pexels.com/photo/pride-month-gathering-2430945/

Goda Morgan. (2023, October 6). Parents leading their little son by the hands along the beach. [Image]. Pexels. https://www.pexels.com/photo/parents-leading-their-little-son-by-the-hands-along-the-beach-18649776/

Julia Avamotive. (2019, May 5). Woman lying on flowers. [Image]. Pexels. https://www.pexels.com/photo/woman-lying-on-flowers-1070967/

Julia M. Cameron. (2020, April 13). Woman in pink and yellow crew neck t-shirt holding brown notebook. [Image]. Pexels. https://www.pexels.com/photo/woman-in-pink-and-yellow-crew-neck-t-shirt-holding-brown-notebook-4143801/

Julia Taubitz. (2021, July 26). Woman in black tank top covering her face with her hands. [Image]. Unsplash. https://unsplash.com/photos/woman-in-black-tank-top-covering-her-face-with-her-hands-tZqYudVcsP0

Kampus Production. (2021, April 26). Men holding their surfboards. [Image]. Pexels. https://www.pexels.com/photo/men-holding-their-surfboards-7659067/

Karolina Grabowska. (2021, May 22). Person holding a book. [Image]. Pexels. https://www.pexels.com/photo/person-holding-a-book-8005552/

Kindel Media. (2021, June 30). Man in a pink shirt sitting beside a teenager crying. [Image]. Pexels. https://www.pexels.com/photo/man-in-a-pink-shirt-sitting-beside-a-teenager-crying-8550682/

Kindel Media. (2021, June 30). Woman in blue shirt talking to a young man in white shirt. [Image]. Pexels. https://www.pexels.com/photo/woman-in-blue-shirt-talking-to-a-young-man-in-white-shirt-8550841/

Maria Orlova. (2020, July 24). Confident woman standing with wineglass and cigarette. [Image]. Pexels. https://www.pexels.com/photo/confident-woman-standing-with-wineglass-and-cigarette-4947275/

Monstera Production. (2021, March 12). Faceless people scolding discontent black girl. [Image].

Pexels. https://www.pexels.com/photo/faceless-people-scolding-discontent-black-girl-7114755/

Polina Tankilevitch. (2021, January 16). A woman in black tube bodysuit holding the tape measure wrapped around her waist. [Image]. Pexels. https://www.pexels.com/photo/a-woman-in-black-tube-bodysuit-holding-the-tape-measure-wrapped-around-her-waist-6516061/

Polina Zimmerman. (2020, March 18). Young woman talking with therapist. [Image]. Pexels. https://www.pexels.com/photo/young-woman-talking-with-therapist-3958461/

Ron Lach. (2021, November 27). Teenage boy in yellow raincoat with head in hands in forest. [Image]. Pexels. https://www.pexels.com/photo/teenage-boy-in-yellow-raincoat-with-head-in-hands-in-forest-10366333/

Shvets production. (2021, February 27). Overweight woman smiling in sportswear with raised arms. [Image]. Pexels. https://www.pexels.com/photo/overweight-smiling-woman-in-sportswear-with-raised-arms-6975391/

Printed by Amazon Italia Logistica S.r.l.
Torrazza Piemonte (TO), Italy

64696118R00098